TWO-

SETTLE

LINE
Leeds-Settle-Carlisle

James Wood

*L*eading *E*dge™
press and publishing

First edition published by White Frog Productions, 1989.
ISBN 0 9514526 0 6

This edition published by Leading Edge Press & Publishing Ltd,
The Old Chapel, Burtersett, Hawes, North Yorkshire, DL8 3PB.
☎ (0969) 667566

**A CIP Catalogue record for this book is available from the
British Library.**

ISBN 0 948135 37 9

Edited by Barbara Allen
Maps by Nick Bagguley
Network map on pages 46/47 by Ruth Abbott
Cover design by Barbara Drew
Illustrations by Ruth Abbott and Barbara Drew
Design and type by Leading Edge Press & Publishing Ltd
Printed and bound in Great Britain by Ebenezer Baylis and Son Ltd, Worcester

Foreword

THE Friends of the Settle–Carlisle Line first became involved with the line in 1981 when the route was threatened with closure. Under pressure from around 22,000 petitioners, the Secretary of State for Transport announced in April 1989 that the closure proposals would not be implemented. He looked instead to all interested parties to work together with British Rail to promote and develop the line to ensure its successful future so that the case for closure would not re-emerge.

Although this guide has been written commencing and terminating at Leeds, it can be used just as easily joining or departing at any point on the route. The two-way journey can easily be achieved in one day on the modern Class 156 Supersprinter.

For those riding on the Settle line for the first time it will soon become obvious that this is no ordinary journey — passing through lowland valleys and the dramatic hill country of the Pennines before descending to the fertile Eden valley through to Carlisle. In all, 113 miles of scenic splendour with the train providing a perfect vantage from which to appreciate the fine views. Enjoy your journey.

Michael Glyn Owen
Chairman, Friends of the Settle–Carlisle Line

Author's note
The first edition of this guide was produced in 1988-89 during a period of great uncertainty about the future of the Settle and Carlisle line. Now, in 1993, notwithstanding the general uncertainty surrounding the government's privatisation ideas, we live in happier times for this railway. Changes are under way; repairs and improvements are being carried out. A new edition of the guide is therefore needed and here it is — updated, with extra material, a complete redesign of the pages and an improved format. I hope it will help you enjoy your journey over England's greatest historical scenic railway route.

A History of the Line

The 113-mile railway between Leeds, Settle and Carlisle was built in the nineteenth century heyday of railways and constructed, in stages, over a period of 30 years.

At that time, long before British Rail was established, railways were developed by separate companies — often competing to carry the available passengers and freight. The first section of the Leeds-Settle-Carlisle route opened in 1846, from Leeds to Shipley, part of the Leeds-Bradford line. Soon after opening, this line was leased by the Midland Railway Company, and in 1847 the line was extended from Shipley to Skipton. With its headquarters in Derby, the Midland Railway had been formed in 1844 by the amalgamation of three railway companies in the Midlands, and its expansion was already taking it far beyond its Midlands home. The Leeds -Shipley-Skipton line was continued through Hellifield to Clapham and Ingleton in 1849, and from Clapham to Lancaster in 1850. This building was carried out by the North Western Railway (called the Little North Western to distinguish it from the much larger London and North Western Railway). The Midland soon made an agreement to run its trains over the Little North Western's system, later taking the company over.

Midland passengers from the south were now able to travel as far as Lancaster to change onto the West Coast Main Line for Carlisle and Scotland.

Improvements seemed likely in 1861 when a better connection from the Midland Railway could be made onto trains for Carlisle and beyond by using the newly opened London and North Western line from Ingleton, north to Low Gill on the West Coast Main Line. This was a shorter journey compared with travelling via Lancaster. Midland passengers from Leeds or south of it could now travel to Ingleton and connect onto a train to Carlisle or further to Scotland. But here was a difficulty since connecting services at Ingleton were very poor. Indeed, at first, passengers had to walk between the Midland and London and North Western companies' stations there, but even after both companies started using the same station connections continued to be poor.

Midland passengers usually had to change not only at Ingleton but soon after at Tebay as well. The Midland was never able to run through trains to Carlisle and Scotland over the London and North Western system, and its complaints brought little improvement. Quite simply the London and North Western wanted people to travel their whole journey over its own metals and was not interested in improving travel for Midland passengers. The Midland's desire to run trains through to Carlisle remained unfulfilled.

Further south the Midland was also having difficulties with access to London. From 1852 it had an agreement with the London and North Western Railway to run trains via Rugby into Euston station, but its trains encountered many delays. So from 1858 it ran them via Hitchin over the Great Northern Railway to Kings Cross station. This was not a happy arrangement either, and consequently the Midland built its own line, extending south from Bedford to a terminus at St Pancras, which opened in 1868.

The Midland's solution to the strained relations further north was likewise to build its own route. Authorised by Act of Parliament in 1866, the 72 $\frac{1}{2}$ mile Settle and Carlisle railway would allow the Midland to run over its own metals from a new junction two miles south of Settle to Petteril Bridge junction, just outside Carlisle, and thence over the North Eastern Railway's line into Carlisle Citadel station.

There was also to be a six-mile branch to Hawes. The possibility of this rival route being developed assisted negotiation between the Midland and the London and North Western companies. Agreement was reached for the Midland to run trains over the West Coast Main Line into Carlisle, to provide the Anglo-Scottish services it wanted, and parliamentary consent was sought to abandon the now unneeded Settle and Carlisle railway. Alas for the Midland, Parliament refused to let the Settle and Carlisle route be given up, so the Midland was obliged to build the line it did not want and which we now know as England's most spectacular main line route.

Building begins

Parliament's refusal to allow the abandonment of the Settle and Carlisle railway came in April 1869. The Midland Railway started construction in the autumn of that year, and the work was let in four contracts for the main line and one for the Hawes branch.

This was the last British railway to be built in traditional fashion, employing thousands of men, hundreds of horses, but none of the earth-moving machinery that soon afterwards became available. Much of the route was built in remote countryside and many of the workforce came in from outside, to be accommodated in shanty towns along the line they were building. They toiled for nearly seven years, quite often in severe conditions and extreme weather. Some died here of diseases or accidents, as graves and memorials in local churches testify. The result of their years of labour was the completion of the Midland Railway's own route from London St Pancras to Carlisle.

The line was engineered so as to avoid speed restrictions due to tight bends or severe gradients. There are continuing steep gradients, of course, but never greater than one in 100, which compares favourably with the one in 75 at Shap, not far away on the London and North Western's west coast main line. As the railway was intended for main line expresses speeding between cities in England and Scotland, not as a rural branch line, it followed the best route from an engineering viewpoint between Settle and Carlisle, without wandering far to serve towns and villages on the way. Indeed in the remoter parts of the journey settlements are non-existent. However, where appropriate, local stations were constructed, though they were not the reason for building the line, and a few of them were at a distance from the places whose names they bore. The railway overcomes the difficult terrain with its 22 viaducts, 14 tunnels, numerous smaller bridges and many cuttings and embankments. Over 16 miles of it are at more than a thousand feet above sea level. In the days of steam the gradients were a challenge, particularly the Long Drag — the climb northwards from Settle Junction up to Blea Moor — and the shorter, but equally steep, climb southwards from Crosby Garrett up to Ais Gill.

The Settle and Carlisle railway opened for goods traffic on August 1, 1875 and for passenger services on May 1, 1876. The Hawes branch opened to passengers on October 1, 1878. Even this branch, six miles of single track descending from Hawes Junction (now named Garsdale) to Hawes at an average gradient of about one in 80, had one tunnel and two viaducts. From Hawes, the North Eastern Railway continued the line down Wensleydale to Northallerton on the east coast main line. This was the only branch on the Settle and Carlisle railway and it allowed connections both local and longer-distance.

An architectural unity is given to the railway by the design of most of its station buildings, repeated the length of the line in different types of stone, and occasionally brick. Houses for employees are also in characteristic style and may be seen near stations and in other places near the line. The bridges and viaducts seem to fit naturally into their landscapes.

Some of the activity, and a lot of the employment associated with the railway in earlier times, have now disappeared. Many signal boxes have been removed, no longer needed with modern signalling systems. Most of the sidings at stations, quarries and other rural industries have now been lifted and a lot of the stations are now unstaffed. Yet the essential railway remains to be travelled on and enjoyed.

The opening of the Settle and Carlisle railway in 1876 completed the Midland Railway's Leeds–Carlisle route begun 30 years earlier. On this 113-mile route the railway follows the valleys of the Aire, Ribble and Eden, the last two conveniently oriented north to south. Near the middle there is a relatively level section through upland terrain, rich in viaducts and tunnels.

Beginning in Leeds, the line climbs gently along the Aire valley for some 35 miles. At first heavily built-up and industrial, the landscape gradually becomes greener with fields punctuated by towns and villages. By the time we pass from the Aire valley into the Ribble valley, just before Hellifield, it has become notably rural. The Ribble is followed for 20 miles up to Blea Moor. After Settle Junction, with the start of the Long Drag, it is noticeable how the gradient steepens while the countryside becomes bleaker with moorland and hills replacing the fields. Much of the route is now at a gradient of one in 100 until Blea Moor is reached. Then for ten miles the line runs pretty level — enabled to do so by long tunnels cutting through the hills and viaducts across valleys, all of which keeps the railway high above Dentdale and Garsdale, until the line's summit is passed at Ais Gill. The rest of the journey, nearly 50 miles, is a long descent of the Eden valley, starting with a ten mile stretch through Mallerstang Common down to Crosby Garrett — much of it at one in 100. The countryside then becomes less wild and more homely and wooded, until the end of the journey is reached at the Border city of Carlisle.

The line opens

With the opening of the Settle and Carlisle railway on May 1, 1876 the Midland Railway achieved its ambition of a route from London to Carlisle. Expresses were run between St Pancras and Carlisle, continuing, by arrangement with two Scottish companies, to reach Glasgow via the Glasgow and South Western Railway; and Edinburgh via the North British Railway. Local stopping trains were provided as well. The Midland's route from London to Scotland was longer than the rival west coast and east coast routes and its journey times were slower, but it stood ahead of other companies in provision of passenger comforts.

In those days railway companies provided three classes of passenger travel, but in 1875 the Midland had pioneered the abolition of second class, upgrading the old third class by providing cushioned seats instead of wooden ones. The year before, the Midland had introduced Pullman cars from the USA into Britain, offering luxury travel to its passengers. From the start Pullman cars were run over the Settle and Carlisle, and sleeping cars ran on overnight trains.

In 1876 the Midland's London to Glasgow service took $10\,{}^3/_4$ hours for the trip, while a journey between Leeds and Carlisle varied from under three hours, on a train with a couple of stops, to over five on one calling at all stations. With the opening of the Hawes branch two years later, three trains ran in each direction connecting Hawes Junction with stations in Wensleydale along to Northallerton on the East Coast Main Line.

Services developed and timings improved over the years. Through trains were run, for instance, from Manchester to Hellifield then over the Settle and Carlisle line to Scottish destinations. Through coaches operated serving places such as Bristol, Stranraer, Aberdeen and Inverness. Train services were probably at their best in the early years of this century up until the First World War. The decline set in in the 1920s as the motor car and bus became more widespread. Most British railways were grouped into four large companies in 1923, when the Midland became part of the London Midland and Scottish Railway, as did its erstwhile rival on the route to Scotland, the London and North Western Railway. In the following years the Settle and Carlisle route assumed a lesser importance, as main line services were concentrated on the west coast route over Shap. Fewer through coaches were run, but there were still fast trains between London and Scotland over the Settle and Carlisle line. The daytime trains from St Pancras to Glasgow and Edinburgh were now named the *Thames–Clyde* and the *Thames–Forth* expresses, the latter being later renamed *The Waverley*. Sleeping car services continued, and so of course did local trains.

After nationalisation of the railways in 1948, services on this route continued much the same as before, but closures were starting. A few stations closed in the 1950s and train services on connecting lines were withdrawn. The Northallerton passenger trains from Garsdale were withdrawn in 1954, leaving the branch only open as far as Hawes, and this section closed five years later. Blackburn–Hellifield services ceased in 1962; the Ilkley and Colne branches from Skipton closed in 1965 and 1970 respectively. Indeed the closure of the whole Settle and Carlisle railway was foreshadowed as early as 1963 in Dr Beeching's report *The Reshaping of British Railways*. The following year the government rejected this closure proposal.

Nonetheless twelve more stations closed in 1970 and freight services were gradually withdrawn from the line.

The Waverley, the St Pancras–Edinburgh express, had ceased to run in 1968, while *The Thames–Clyde Express* between St Pancras and Glasgow lost its name in 1975, being withdrawn the following year (which, by a nice irony, was the Settle and Carlisle's centenary). In 1977 the last St Pancras–Scotland service disappeared when the London–Glasgow overnight train was withdrawn. After this the only services on the Settle and Carlisle line were Nottingham–Leeds–Carlisle–Glasgow trains. North of Settle they stopped only at Appleby. No other stations were open so there were of course no local stopping services.

1982 was a low point in the line's fortunes since the Nottingham–Glasgow trains were rerouted away from it and the only trains to serve the line were then a twice daily service in each direction between Leeds and Carlisle, with no Sunday trains. Despite the run-down of services to this level, British Rail maintained it had no plans to close the line.

But, to see a glimmer of hope for a more cheerful future, we have to look back to 1974, when a ramblers' group persuaded British Rail to run a day excursion train to Garsdale, a station closed four years before, for the benefit of walkers. The success of this led to the establishment of DalesRail in 1975, whereby excursion trains were run at weekends so that walkers in West Yorkshire could get to normally-closed stations on the Settle and Carlisle railway, have a day walking and then return in the evening. DalesRail was successful and expanded, with trains running additionally from Lancashire via Hellifield, and also continuing up to Carlisle. As it developed, DalesRail allowed town dwellers to reach the country and country dwellers to make the opposite journey for a day in town. Connecting buses ran from some stations too. Some 6,000 used these trains each summer. The 'closed' stations served were the ones reopened fully in 1986. Due to these reopenings DalesRail is no longer needed from West Yorkshire but it still operates as a BR service on some summer weekends from Stockport and Blackpool, running via the Blackburn–Hellifield line, then north to Carlisle.

The line is saved

The long decline in rail services over the Settle and Carlisle line led a lot of people to think that British Rail was preparing it for closure. This was always denied, but many were unconvinced. Neglected maintenance in recent years meant that there were costly repairs to be undertaken, Ribblehead viaduct being the most publicised case. This allegedly had only a few more years' life left in it, or might cost huge sums to replace or repair it — £6 million was a possibility cited in 1981.

Against this background of poor train services, low maintenance of the route and uncertain prospects for the railway, the Friends of the Settle–Carlisle Line Association was founded in 1981, to campaign for the future of the line. In August 1983 British Rail officially notified its intention to seek closure of the line. Soon after this a Joint Action Committee was established to bring together the efforts of the Friends, the Railway Development Association and Transport 2000 in the fight against closure and for the development of the line. The official closure notice was first issued in December 1983, but British Rail needed two more attempts before it was certain the notice was legally correct.

Meanwhile, objections to closure were received from 22,265 people and one dog. An extra train had to be run in high summer in 1984 between Leeds and Carlisle in response to demand. 1985 saw additional summer trains, including one on Sundays again. Hearings into closure objections were held by the Transport Users' Consultative Committees in March 1986. In July eight of the stations which had closed in 1970 were reopened to additional train services. These were stations used by DalesRail excursion trains over the past 11 years and their reopening for daily use thus did not pose insuperable problems. The additional trains were well used. The Transport Users' Consultative Committees reported in December 1986 firmly rejecting British Rail's case for closure, but the final decision lay with the Minister and his decision was a long time arriving.

Meanwhile patronage had grown from 93,000 passengers in 1983, who used the rump service of two daily trains in each direction between Leeds and Carlisle, to nearly half a million in 1988 on the five trains each way, which called additionally at the eight reopened stations. One of the options being floated at this time was privatisation of the line and when the Minister at last announced a decision, in May 1988, he said, despite all the evidence, that he was minded to consent to closure but wanted British Rail to find a private buyer for the line. He also wanted to hear new evidence from users of the trains in view of the additional stations and train services now available. In September, now with over 32,000 objections lodged, the Transport Users' Consultative Committees held further hearings, reporting in December still firmly against closure. No private buyer had emerged for the railway. A test repair on part of Ribblehead viaduct indicated, as anti-closure campaigners had long believed, that the total repair costs for this viaduct would be much lower than British Rail had been suggesting. Then on April 11, 1989 the Minister announced that he was refusing closure for the Settle and Carlisle railway. Privatisation was out but he asked British Rail to consider involving the private sector in marketing and operating the line. Relief and rejoicing ended the long years of uncertainty — a period, which from British Rail's first announced intention to seek closure up to the Minister's refusal, had lasted nearly as long as the Midland Railway took to construct the line.

The future

And so the Leeds–Settle–Carlisle line still runs. Indeed, the Settle and Carlisle section must now have its most intensive passenger service ever, with, basically, six trains a day (three on summer Sundays) in each direction, calling at all stations.

What are the prospects for the future of this railway? Following the Minister's reprieve, and with the certainty that there is to be a future, both British Rail and other interests set to work. Strangely, the line really was closed down in October 1989, but only for a fortnight, between Settle and Appleby, to allow repair works to be carried out at several locations. This included laying a waterproof membrane under the track bed on Ribblehead viaduct to prevent water ingress into the arches and piers. This was only the start of a repair programme continuing after the line was reopened. Platforms at some stations were lengthened to take four-car Sprinter trains.

The Friends of the Settle–Carlisle Line have continued to support the line. Under their station adoption scheme, begun a few years before, many stations have been painted, platform seats installed and gardens planted and maintained. The Friends have also restored the unused Midland Railway signal box at Armathwaite, because it is a good example of its kind and, being set back from the line, it can easily be seen from passing trains. At Appleby, the Round Table has reinstated the water tank and water column to service steam locomotives on the regular steam excursions over the route. In 1991, the local authorities declared the railway from Hellifield to Carlisle a conservation area which will offer some protection to buildings and structures and may open the door to grants. The Settle and Carlisle Railway Trust, a charitable body, was established in 1990 to help in restoring structures along the line and in promoting appreciation of it.

And what of the future beyond the next tunnel and viaduct? It is hoped that improvements in facilities and trains services will continue. The 26 $1/_4$ miles from Leeds to Skipton are being electrified, a project due for completion in 1994. A northbound platform was completed in the summer of 1993 at Ribblehead station. The future of historic station buildings at Hellifield is still unknown. Restoration of trains running via Hellifield from Manchester and north Lancashire onto the Settle and Carlisle railway will be a possibility when the Hellifield–Blackburn line is fully reopened. Another travel opportunity which many believe needs to be restored is the train service between Glasgow and West Yorkshire and East Midlands. Not since 1982 have there been long-distance trains on the Settle and Carlisle route, though of course these are the trains it was built for, and the reappearance of the Glasgow—Carlisle–Leeds–Nottingham services would be welcome. Sunday trains have returned in summer but not yet all the year round. Regular freight traffic has not used the line for years and its return would be welcome.

The Settle and Carlisle line has a secure place within the railway network and — provided the integrity of the system as a whole is not a victim of the government's privatisation plans — hopefully it will continue to enjoy improvements and development in the future.

Useful addresses

If you have enjoyed your journey on this railway, you may be interested in some related organisations. Here is a list of some:

Friends of the Settle-Carlisle Line

Founded under the longer title of Friends of the Settle-Carlisle Line Association in 1981, it campaigned for the retention of the line and now works for its future development. Members receive a quarterly newspaper with information about the line. Membership costs £6 a year and this should be sent to the Membership Secretary, 16 Pickard Court, Leeds LS15 9AY.

Settle and Carlisle Railway Trust

A charity founded in 1990, its objects are to assist in restoring some of the structures along the line and to promote public appreciation of it. Donations are welcomed and further details can be had from the Trust at The Railway Station, Broughton Road, Skipton, North Yorkshire BD23 1RT

Wensleydale Railway Association

Established in 1990, the Association is investigating the possible reinstatement of passenger trains between Garsdale, on the Settle and Carlisle line, and Northallerton on the East Coast Main Line. Of this 40–mile railway, 22 miles from Northallerton to Redmire were in use until the end of 1992 for quarry traffic, while 18 miles from Redmire via Hawes to Garsdale are closed with the track lifted. Members get regular newsletters with the latest information about reopening possibilities. Membership costs £5 a year and this should be sent to Membership Administration, 19 Springwell Lane, Northallerton, North Yorkshire DL7 8QJ.

Ribble Valley Rail

This organisation was set up in 1987 to press for the improvement and development of rail services on the Hellifield–Blackburn line. Summer Saturday services started on part of the line in 1990, between Blackburn and Clitheroe and DalesRail services use the whole line on some summer Sundays, but a full reopening to daily trains has yet to come. Members receive a quarterly newsletter to keep them up to date. Membership costs £2.50 a year and this should be sent to the Membership Secretary, 55 Bank Head Lane, Hoghton, Preston PR5 0AB.

Northern Viaduct Trust

Set up in 1989 this Trust has restored Smardale Gill viaduct, visible from the Settle and Carlisle line between Kirkby Stephen and Crosby Garrett. Further details about the work of the Trust can be had from the Chairman, Northern Viaduct Trust, 22 West Street, Gargrave, North Yorkshire BD23 3RD.

Further reading

Many books and maps are available which cover his railway.

If you are looking for a short history of the line try *Settle to Carlisle* by W R Mitchell and David Joy, published by Dalesman Books. Or if you want a longer account look for *Midland Railway North of Leeds* by Peter E Baughan, published by David and Charles. For the story of the successful campaign to save the railway with an account of the issues behind rail closures read *The Line that Refused to Die* by Stan Abbott and Alan Whitehouse, published by Leading Edge Press and Publishing.

A useful series of maps including the railway and its surroundings is the Landranger Series published by the Ordnance Survey at 1:50 000 scale, about 1 $1/_4$ inches to the mile. Seven maps cover the whole route:

Sheet 85	Carlisle and the Solway Firth
Sheet 86	Haltwhistle, Bewcastle and Alston area
Sheet 90	Penrith, Keswick and Ambleside area
Sheet 91	Appleby-in-Westmorland area
Sheet 98	Wensleydale and Upper Wharfedale
Sheet 103	Blackburn, Burnley and surrounding area
Sheet 104	Leeds, Bradford and Harrogate area

How to use this guide

The Two Way Guide to the Settle Line consists of two parts. Your direction of travel — are you going towards Leeds or Carlisle? — is what determines which end of the guide you will use. Make sure you are reading the appropriate part.

The guide is written from the viewpoint of a passenger facing the direction of travel and following the journey reading <u>up the page</u> from bottom to top. The railway is indicated diagrammatically with every quarter mile marked like a sleeper between the rails, and every full mile shown with its number. Five miles of the route are on each page, with features of interest shown on the line to the left and right nearby.

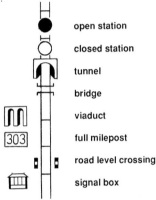

●	open station
○	closed station
	tunnel
	bridge
⋔	viaduct
303	full milepost
▪ ▪	road level crossing
�	signal box

The Midland Railway placed mileposts every quarter mile to indicate the distance to London St Pancras. Excepting about a mile outside Carlisle and Leeds, they are mostly visible, on the right going towards Carlisle or the left going towards Leeds.

Usually they are of cast iron on posts three or four feet high, beside the line or sometimes attached to buildings. The full miles have two oblong faces, angled to be seen from each direction, and the fractional distances have three faces which are also readable form both directions. Gradient posts can also be seen. They are on the opposite side of the tracks to the mileposts and are much smaller.

Kirkstall Junction signal box

This was never a junction but the signal box served goods lines.

Bridge crossing the Leeds and Liverpool Canal

(ARMLEY CANAL ROAD)

110 feet above sea level
Leeds 1 3/4 miles
Carlisle 111 1/4 miles

Armley Canal Road station closed in 1965 — buildings remain at street level.
Holbeck Low Level station closed in 1958, as did Holbeck High Level station above it. Nothing remains of them today. The high level station was on the branch to Leeds Central, not far away to the right. This was Leeds' other main station, closed in 1967 with rationalisation of services.

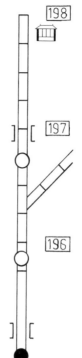

198

197

196

For over 30 miles the railway follows the Aire valley, as doe the Leeds and Liverpool Cana completed in 1816. The Rive Aire and the canal are often seen from the railway, which crosses the river 12 times and the canal four.

to Harrogate

Wortley Junction

(HOLBECK LOW LEVEL)

100 feet above sea level
Leeds 3/4 mile
Carlisle 112 1/4 miles

Bridge crossing the Leeds and Liverpool Canal

LEEDS

110 feet above sea level
Carlisle 113 miles

Trains on this route originally used Leeds Wellington station, opened in 1846 and beyond the present platforms to the right. It was modernised in 1938 with an elegant concourse but is not now used for passengers.

Leeds Town Hall

203

to Ilkley

Woodhouse Bridge — 4 arches crossing the River Aire

Apperley Junction

APPERLEY BRIDGE

200 feet above sea level
Leeds 7 1/2 miles
Carlisle 105 1/2 miles

Apperley Bridge station closed in 1965. It stood just before the road bridge, but no buildings are left. Until 1961 the station was called Apperley Bridge and Rawdon.

Bridge crossing the River Aire

201

CALVERLEY & RODLEY

180 feet above sea level
Leeds 5 3/4 miles
Carlisle 107 1/4 miles

Calverley and Rodley station closed in 1965 and its buildings were later demolished.

Bridge crossing the River Aire

NEWLAY

140 feet above sea level
Leeds 4 3/4 miles
Carlisle 108 1/4 miles

Newlay station closed in 1965. It was located immediately before the road bridge. No buildings now remain. Until 1961 the station was called Newlay and Horsforth.

200

KIRKSTALL FORGE

150 feet above sea level
Leeds 4 miles
Carlisle 109 miles

Kirkstall Forge station closed in 1905. It was straight after the river bridges and nothing remains of it now.

Kirkstall Forge bridges, Lower and Upper, crossing the River Aire

199

Kirkstall Abbey

KIRKSTALL

110 feet above sea level
Leeds 3 1/4 miles
Carlisle 109 3/4 miles

Kirkstall station closed in 1965 and its buildings were later demolished. The station was straight after the road bridge.

198

On the right can be seen the ruins of Kirkstall Abbey, which was founded by the Cistercian Order in 1152 and dissolved under Henry VIII in 1539. It is open to the public.

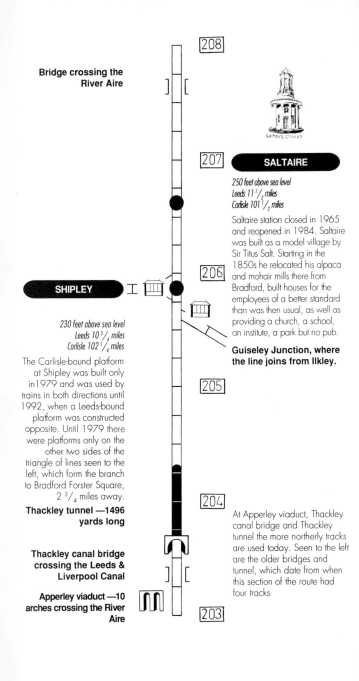

Bridge crossing the River Aire

208

207

Saltaire Church

SALTAIRE

250 feet above sea level
Leeds 11 ¹/₂ miles
Carlisle 101 ¹/₂ miles

Saltaire station closed in 1965 and reopened in 1984. Saltaire was built as a model village by Sir Titus Salt. Starting in the 1850s he relocated his alpaca and mohair mills there from Bradford, built houses for the employees of a better standard than was then usual, as well as providing a church, a school, an institute, a park but no pub.

206

SHIPLEY

230 feet above sea level
Leeds 10 ³/₄ miles
Carlisle 102 ¹/₄ miles

The Carlisle-bound platform at Shipley was built only in 1979 and was used by trains in both directions until 1992, when a Leeds-bound platform was constructed opposite. Until 1979 there were platforms only on the other two sides of the triangle of lines seen to the left, which form the branch to Bradford Forster Square, 2 ³/₄ miles away.

Guiseley Junction, where the line joins from Ilkley.

205

Thackley tunnel —1496 yards long

204

Thackley canal bridge crossing the Leeds & Liverpool Canal

Apperley viaduct —10 arches crossing the River Aire

203

At Apperley viaduct, Thackley canal bridge and Thackley tunnel the more northerly tracks are used today. Seen to the left are the older bridges and tunnel, which date from when this section of the route had four tracks

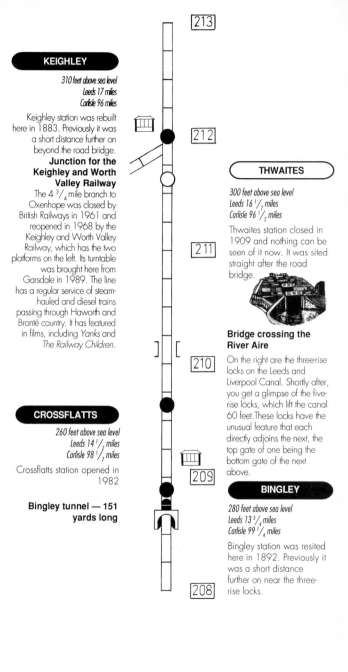

213

KEIGHLEY

310 feet above sea level
Leeds 17 miles
Carlisle 96 miles

Keighley station was rebuilt
here in 1883. Previously it was
a short distance further on
beyond the road bridge.
**Junction for the
Keighley and Worth
Valley Railway**
The 4 $^3/_4$ mile branch to
Oxenhope was closed by
British Railways in 1961 and
reopened in 1968 by the
Keighley and Worth Valley
Railway, which has the two
platforms on the left. Its turntable
was brought here from
Garsdale in 1989. The line
has a regular service of steam-
hauled and diesel trains
passing through Haworth and
Brontë country. It has featured
in films, including *Yanks* and
The Railway Children.

212

THWAITES

300 feet above sea level
Leeds 16 $^1/_2$ miles
Carlisle 96 $^1/_2$ miles

Thwaites station closed in
1909 and nothing can be
seen of it now. It was sited
straight after the road
bridge.

211

**Bridge crossing the
River Aire**

On the right are the three-rise
locks on the Leeds and
Liverpool Canal. Shortly after,
you get a glimpse of the five-
rise locks, which lift the canal
60 feet. These locks have the
unusual feature that each
directly adjoins the next, the
top gate of one being the
bottom gate of the next
above.

210

CROSSFLATTS

260 feet above sea level
Leeds 14 $^1/_2$ miles
Carlisle 98 $^1/_2$ miles

Crossflatts station opened in
1982

**Bingley tunnel — 151
yards long**

209

BINGLEY

280 feet above sea level
Leeds 13 $^3/_4$ miles
Carlisle 99 $^1/_4$ miles

Bingley station was resited
here in 1892. Previously it
was a short distance
further on near the three-
rise locks.

208

KILDWICK & CROSSHILLS

310 feet above sea level
Leeds 21 ³/₄ miles
Carlisle 91 ¹/₄ miles

Kildwick and Crosshills
station was resited
immediately after the road
bridge in 1889. It closed in
1965 and no buildings
remain.
The original station building
was on the left opposite the
signal box.

STEETON & SILSDEN

300 feet above sea level
Leeds 20 miles
Carlisle 93 miles

Steeton and Silsden station
closed in 1965 and reopened
in 1990, when new platforms
were built, with shelters.
Opposite the Leeds-bound
platform is the original station
building.

218

217

216

215

214

213

former junction for Colne was sited just before the road bridge. The line to Colne closed to passengers in 1970. Until then services ran between Skipton, stations in north Lancashire and Manchester. The line remains open from Colne onwards.

223

Skipton by-pass

222

Skipton by-pass

The former Ilkley line crosses on a bridge. Passenger trains ceased in 1965 but as far as Embsay Junction it is still used by goods trains on the Grassington branch serving Swinden quarry, now the end of the line. From Embsay Junction the Yorkshire Dales Railway has reopened the Ilkley line to a run-round loop half a mile beyond Holywell Halt and plans to reopen it as far as Bolton Abbey. Steam-hauled and diesel trains are operated.

Skipton by-pass

SKIPTON

340 feet above sea level
Leeds 26 $^1/_4$ miles
Carlisle 86 $^3/_4$ miles

Originally Skipton station was about a quarter of a mile nearer Leeds. The present station was built in 1876, to cater for increased traffic with the opening of the Settle and Carlisle railway. The disused platforms on the left were used by trains on the Ilkley line.

221

220

Bridge crossing the River Aire

219

Skipton Castle

CONONLEY

310 feet above sea level
Leeds 23 $^1/_4$ miles
Carlisle 89 $^3/_4$ miles

218

Cononley station closed in 1965 and its buildings were later demolished. It reopened in 1988, when shelters were provided on both platforms.

Bell Busk viaduct 7 arches crossing the River Aire.

This is the last of 12 crossings of the River Aire, which rises near Malham, 5 miles north of here.

Two bridges crossing the River Aire then the Leeds and Liverpool Canal.

As you cross the canal, look left and see it crossing the River Aire on the Priest Holme aqueduct. The Leeds and Liverpool Canal, like the railway, has followed the Aire valley from Leeds. With Gargrave as its most northerly point it now leaves the route of the railway to go southwestwards into Lancashire.

GARGRAVE

400 feet above sea level
Leeds 30 miles
Carlisle 83 miles

228

BELL BUSK

480 feet above sea level
Leeds 32 3/4 miles
Carlisle 80 1/4 miles

Bell Busk station closed in 1959. The railway timetable used to advise travellers to Malham to alight here. Half-timbered buildings remain on the right.

227

226

The Pennine Way crosses on a bridge. 250 miles long, it was the first official long-distance footpath and runs from Edale in Derbyshire to Kirk Yetholm in Roxburghshire, (now the Borders Region).

225

224

223 **Bridge crossing the River Aire**

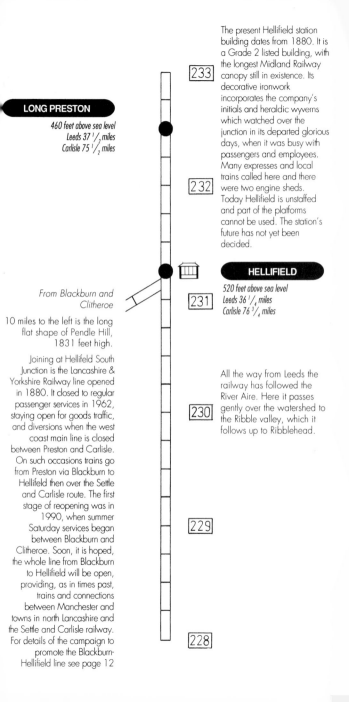

The present Hellifield station building dates from 1880. It is a Grade 2 listed building, with the longest Midland Railway canopy still in existence. Its decorative ironwork incorporates the company's initials and heraldic wyverns which watched over the junction in its departed glorious days, when it was busy with passengers and employees. Many expresses and local trains called here and there were two engine sheds. Today Hellifield is unstaffed and part of the platforms cannot be used. The station's future has not yet been decided.

LONG PRESTON

460 feet above sea level
Leeds 37 $\frac{1}{2}$ miles
Carlisle 75 $\frac{1}{2}$ miles

233

232

231

230

229

228

From Blackburn and Clitheroe

10 miles to the left is the long flat shape of Pendle Hill, 1831 feet high.

Joining at Hellifield South Junction is the Lancashire & Yorkshire Railway line opened in 1880. It closed to regular passenger services in 1962, staying open for goods traffic, and diversions when the west coast main line is closed between Preston and Carlisle. On such occasions trains go from Preston via Blackburn to Hellifield then over the Settle and Carlisle route. The first stage of reopening was in 1990, when summer Saturday services began between Blackburn and Clitheroe. Soon, it is hoped, the whole line from Blackburn to Hellifield will be open, providing, as in times past, trains and connections between Manchester and towns in north Lancashire and the Settle and Carlisle railway. For details of the campaign to promote the Blackburn-Hellifield line see page 12

HELLIFIELD

520 feet above sea level
Leeds 36 $\frac{1}{4}$ miles
Carlisle 76 $\frac{3}{4}$ miles

All the way from Leeds the railway has followed the River Aire. Here it passes gently over the watershed to the Ribble valley, which it follows up to Ribblehead.

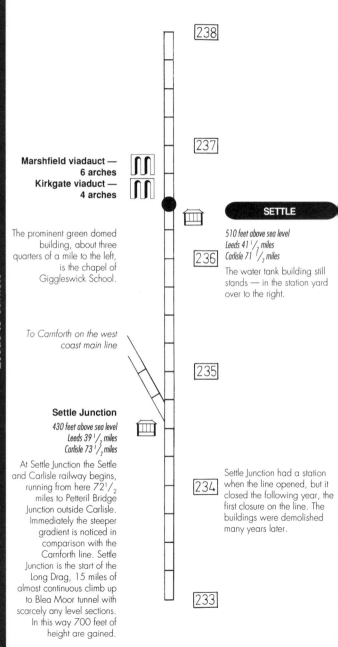

238

237

**Marshfield viaduct —
6 arches
Kirkgate viaduct —
4 arches**

The prominent green domed
building, about three
quarters of a mile to the left,
is the chapel of
Giggleswick School.

SETTLE

510 feet above sea level
Leeds 41 1/2 miles
Carlisle 71 1/2 miles

The water tank building still
stands — in the station yard
over to the right.

236

*To Carnforth on the west
coast main line*

235

Settle Junction
430 feet above sea level
Leeds 39 1/2 miles
Carlisle 73 1/2 miles

At Settle Junction the Settle
and Carlisle railway begins,
running from here 72 1/2
miles to Petteril Bridge
Junction outside Carlisle.
Immediately the steeper
gradient is noticed in
comparison with the
Carnforth line. Settle
Junction is the start of the
Long Drag, 15 miles of
almost continuous climb up
to Blea Moor tunnel with
scarcely any level sections.
In this way 700 feet of
height are gained.

234

Settle Junction had a station
when the line opened, but it
closed the following year, the
first closure on the line. The
buildings were demolished
many years later.

233

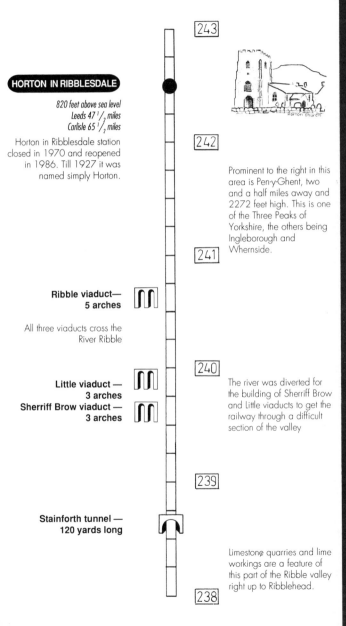

243

HORTON IN RIBBLESDALE

820 feet above sea level
Leeds 47 1/2 miles
Carlisle 65 1/2 miles

Horton in Ribblesdale station closed in 1970 and reopened in 1986. Till 1927 it was named simply Horton.

Horton church

242

Prominent to the right in this area is Pen-y-Ghent, two and a half miles away and 2272 feet high. This is one of the Three Peaks of Yorkshire, the others being Ingleborough and Whernside.

241

Ribble viaduct—
5 arches

All three viaducts cross the River Ribble

240

Little viaduct —
3 arches
Sherriff Brow viaduct —
3 arches

The river was diverted for the building of Sherriff Brow and Little viaducts to get the railway through a difficult section of the valley

239

Stainforth tunnel —
120 yards long

Limestone quarries and lime workings are a feature of this part of the Ribble valley right up to Ribblehead.

238

23

Ribblehead viaduct — 24 arches

Ribblehead is by far the longest viaduct on the route, taking the railway from the Ribble valley to cut through mountainous terrain towards the Eden valley. In 1985 nearly a mile of track was singled to reduce wear and tear on the viaduct.

Ingleborough, 2373 feet high and 3 miles away, is prominent to the left. It is seen well from Ribblehead viaduct.

Ribblehead Viaduct

248

247

246

245

244

243

Single track section begins

RIBBLEHEAD

1030 feet above sea level
Leeds 52 1/4 miles
Carlisle 60 3/4 miles

Ribblehead station closed in 1970 and reopened in 1986 for southbound trains only. The northbound platform had been removed when a branch for the quarry on the left was built. A new one opened in summer 1993, the product of co-operation between BR, FOSCL and the Rural Development Commission. The station in times past has been a centre for the local scattered community and a reporting point for meteorological data. The stationmaster regularly sent in details such as rainfall and windspeed.

During the railway construction period shanty towns were built for the workforce and their families. Some of these were in the Ribblehead area, below the viaduct and around Blea Moor tunnel, but little trace remains of them today. A tramway was built from the road at Ribblehead to carry materials for the building of Blea Moor tunnel, and parts of its trackbed can still be seen.

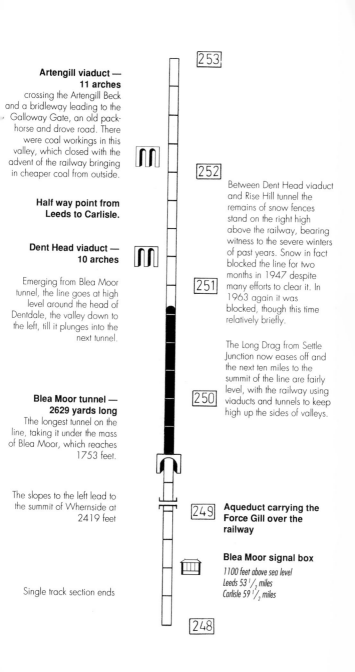

**Artengill viaduct —
11 arches**

crossing the Artengill Beck and a bridleway leading to the Galloway Gate, an old pack-horse and drove road. There were coal workings in this valley, which closed with the advent of the railway bringing in cheaper coal from outside.

**Half way point from
Leeds to Carlisle.**

**Dent Head viaduct —
10 arches**

Emerging from Blea Moor tunnel, the line goes at high level around the head of Dentdale, the valley down to the left, till it plunges into the next tunnel.

**Blea Moor tunnel —
2629 yards long**

Tthe longest tunnel on the line, taking it under the mass of Blea Moor, which reaches 1753 feet.

The slopes to the left lead to the summit of Whernside at 2419 feet

Single track section ends

253

252

251

250

249

248

Between Dent Head viaduct and Rise Hill tunnel the remains of snow fences stand on the right high above the railway, bearing witness to the severe winters of past years. Snow in fact blocked the line for two months in 1947 despite many efforts to clear it. In 1963 again it was blocked, though this time relatively briefly.

The Long Drag from Settle Junction now eases off and the next ten miles to the summit of the line are fairly level, with the railway using viaducts and tunnels to keep high up the sides of valleys.

**Aqueduct carrying the
Force Gill over the
railway**

Blea Moor signal box
1100 feet above sea level
Leeds 53 ¹/₂ miles
Carlisle 59 ¹/₂ miles

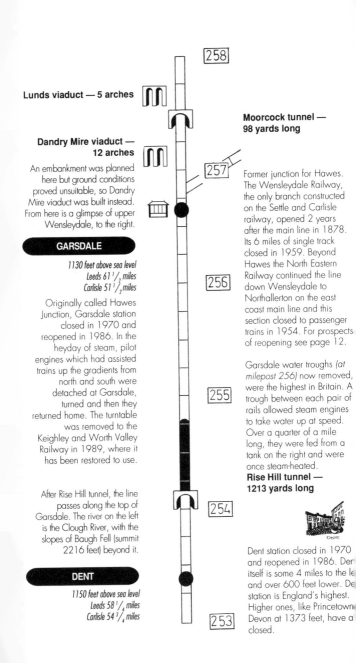

Lunds viaduct — 5 arches

258

**Moorcock tunnel —
98 yards long**

**Dandry Mire viaduct —
12 arches**

An embankment was planned
here but ground conditions
proved unsuitable, so Dandry
Mire viaduct was built instead.
From here is a glimpse of upper
Wensleydale, to the right.

257

Former junction for Hawes.
The Wensleydale Railway,
the only branch constructed
on the Settle and Carlisle
railway, opened 2 years
after the main line in 1878.
Its 6 miles of single track
closed in 1959. Beyond
Hawes the North Eastern
Railway continued the line
down Wensleydale to
Northallerton on the east
coast main line and this
section closed to passenger
trains in 1954. For prospects
of reopening see page 12.

GARSDALE

1130 feet above sea level
Leeds 61 ¹/₂ miles
Carlisle 51 ¹/₂ miles

Originally called Hawes
Junction, Garsdale station
closed in 1970 and
reopened in 1986. In the
heyday of steam, pilot
engines which had assisted
trains up the gradients from
north and south were
detached at Garsdale,
turned and then they
returned home. The turntable
was removed to the
Keighley and Worth Valley
Railway in 1989, where it
has been restored to use.

256

255

Garsdale water troughs *(at
milepost 256)* now removed,
were the highest in Britain. A
trough between each pair of
rails allowed steam engines
to take water up at speed.
Over a quarter of a mile
long, they were fed from a
tank on the right and were
once steam-heated.
**Rise Hill tunnel —
1213 yards long**

After Rise Hill tunnel, the line
passes along the top of
Garsdale. The river on the left
is the Clough River, with the
slopes of Baugh Fell (summit
2216 feet) beyond it.

254

Dent station closed in 1970
and reopened in 1986. Den
itself is some 4 miles to the le
and over 600 feet lower. De
station is England's highest.
Higher ones, like Princetown
Devon at 1373 feet, have a
closed.

DENT

1150 feet above sea level
Leeds 58 ¹/₄ miles
Carlisle 54 ³/₄ miles

253

The slopes of Wild Boar Fell, rising to 2324 feet, are on the left.

263

262

Having passed the summit of the route at Ais Gill , the line now begins the long descent down the Eden valley to Carlisle. Initially steep through Mallerstang Common down to Crosby Garrett, the gradients thereafter become gentler. The railway at first runs high up the valley side with the infant River Eden down to the right. Beyond it the land rises sharply up to Mallerstang Edge, whose summit is High Seat at 2328 feet.

261

**Ais Gill viaduct —
4 arches**

The waterfall on the right is on the Hell Gill Beck, one of the sources of the River Eden.

260

Ais Gill summit
1169 feet above sea level
Leeds 64 ³/₄ miles
Carlisle 48 ¹/₄ miles

The signal box formerly here is now preserved at Butterley in Derbyshire by the Midland Railway Trust.

More than a thousand feet higher than both Leeds and Carlisle is the summit of the railway at Ais Gill. A board on the right marks this highest point reached by a railway in England.

259

Ais Gill marks the old county boundary of Yorkshire and Westmorland, and is the watershed of the River Eden, flowing into the Solway, and the River Ure, which flows down Wensleydale and eventually into the North Sea.

**Shotlock Hill tunnel —
106 yards long**

258

Bookcross, Kirkby Stephen

KIRKBY STEPHEN

890 feet above sea level
Leeds 71 1/2 miles
Carlisle 41 1/2 miles

Kirkby Stephen station closed in 1970 and reopened in 1986. Kirkby Stephen itself lies to the right over a mile and half distant and more than 300 feet lower, but had the railway followed a route to run through the town, it would have lost so much height that the gradient from Ais Gill down to there would have been too steep. The former North Eastern Railway's Penrith — Barnard Castle line with a branch to Tebay ran much closer to Kirkby Stephen and had a station there called Kirkby Stephen East, which closed in 1962. Kirkby Stephen station has had several name changes, most recently in 1968 when it was altered from Kirkby Stephen West.

**Birkett tunnel —
424 yards long**

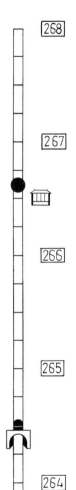

Pendragon Castle

Beside the Eden stands Pendragon Castle. Earlier associated with Uther Pendragon, King Arthur's father, the present castle dates from the twelfth century and was last restored in 1660-61 by Lady Anne Clifford who visited it frequently.

Outhgill, a small village seen just across the river, is the only settlement in Mallerstang Common. Otherwise there are isolated farms and houses. Indeed this section of the line from Garsdale to Kirkby Stephen is the longest never to have had a station.

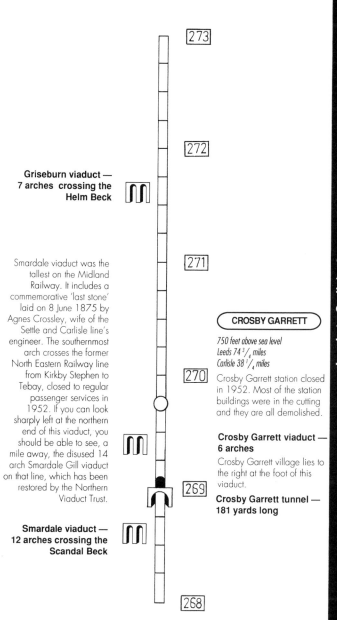

273

272

**Griseburn viaduct —
7 arches crossing the
Helm Beck**

271

Smardale viaduct was the
tallest on the Midland
Railway. It includes a
commemorative 'last stone'
laid on 8 June 1875 by
Agnes Crossley, wife of the
Settle and Carlisle line's
engineer. The southernmost
arch crosses the former
North Eastern Railway line
from Kirkby Stephen to
Tebay, closed to regular
passenger services in
1952. If you can look
sharply left at the northern
end of this viaduct, you
should be able to see, a
mile away, the disused 14
arch Smardale Gill viaduct
on that line, which has been
restored by the Northern
Viaduct Trust.

**Smardale viaduct —
12 arches crossing the
Scandal Beck**

CROSBY GARRETT

750 feet above sea level
Leeds 74 ³/₄ miles
Carlisle 38 ¹/₄ miles

270

Crosby Garrett station closed
in 1952. Most of the station
buildings were in the cutting
and they are all demolished.

**Crosby Garrett viaduct —
6 arches**

Crosby Garrett village lies to
the right at the foot of this
viaduct.

**Crosby Garrett tunnel —
181 yards long**

269

268

29

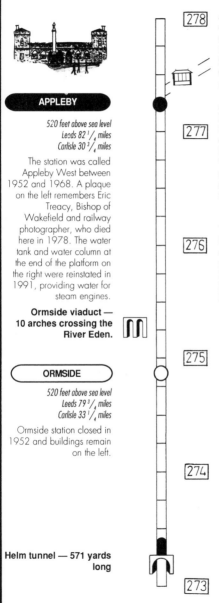

APPLEBY

520 feet above sea level
Leeds 82 1/4 miles
Carlisle 30 3/4 miles

The station was called Appleby West between 1952 and 1968. A plaque on the left remembers Eric Treacy, Bishop of Wakefield and railway photographer, who died here in 1978. The water tank and water column at the end of the platform on the right were reinstated in 1991, providing water for steam engines.

Ormside viaduct — 10 arches crossing the River Eden.

ORMSIDE

520 feet above sea level
Leeds 79 3/4 miles
Carlisle 33 1/4 miles

Ormside station closed in 1952 and buildings remain on the left.

Helm tunnel — 571 yards long

278

277

276

275

274

273

Appleby North Junction connects the Settle and Carlisle line with the former North Eastern Railway line from Penrith to Barnard Castle, which closed to regular passenger services in 1962.
Appleby East station, on that line, was a short distance up the road from the northern end of Appleby station. Some 6 miles, to just beyond Warcop, remain and were used till 1989 to serve an army depot, but the future of this section is uncertain.

The dairy had its own siding between 1930 and 1970, and during this period tankers of milk were sent to London. The slogan 'Milk for London' was displayed on the side of the building.

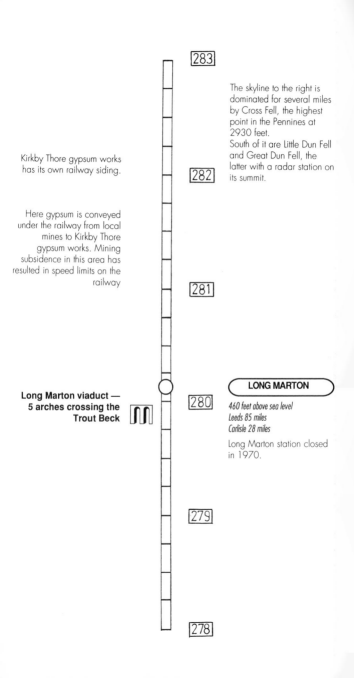

Kirkby Thore gypsum works has its own railway siding.

Here gypsum is conveyed under the railway from local mines to Kirkby Thore gypsum works. Mining subsidence in this area has resulted in speed limits on the railway

Long Marton viaduct — 5 arches crossing the Trout Beck

283

282

The skyline to the right is dominated for several miles by Cross Fell, the highest point in the Pennines at 2930 feet.
South of it are Little Dun Fell and Great Dun Fell, the latter with a radar station on its summit.

281

280

279

278

LONG MARTON

460 feet above sea level
Leeds 85 miles
Carlisle 28 miles

Long Marton station closed in 1970.

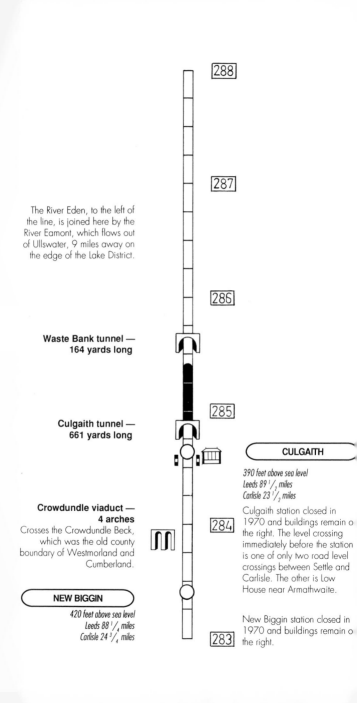

The River Eden, to the left of the line, is joined here by the River Eamont, which flows out of Ullswater, 9 miles away on the edge of the Lake District.

**Waste Bank tunnel —
164 yards long**

**Culgaith tunnel —
661 yards long**

**Crowdundle viaduct —
4 arches**
Crosses the Crowdundle Beck, which was the old county boundary of Westmorland and Cumberland.

⬭ **NEW BIGGIN** ⬭

*420 feet above sea level
Leeds 88 1/4 miles
Carlisle 24 3/4 miles*

[288]

[287]

[286]

[285]

[284]

[283]

⬭ **CULGAITH** ⬭

*390 feet above sea level
Leeds 89 1/2 miles
Carlisle 23 1/2 miles*

Culgaith station closed in 1970 and buildings remain o the right. The level crossing immediately before the station is one of only two road level crossings between Settle and Carlisle. The other is Low House near Armathwaite.

New Biggin station closed in 1970 and buildings remain o the right.

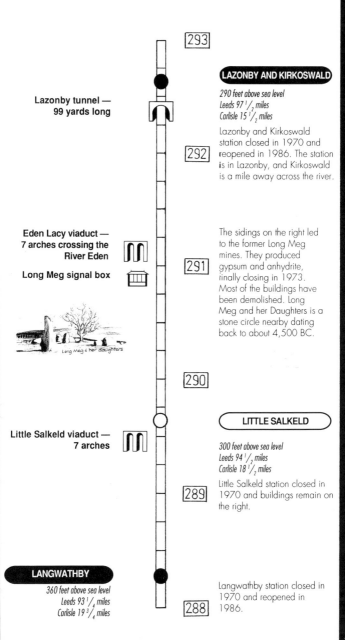

293

292

291

290

289

288

**Lazonby tunnel —
99 yards long**

**Eden Lacy viaduct —
7 arches crossing the
River Eden**

Long Meg signal box

Long Meg & her daughters

**Little Salkeld viaduct —
7 arches**

LAZONBY AND KIRKOSWALD

290 feet above sea level
Leeds 97 1/2 miles
Carlisle 15 1/2 miles

Lazonby and Kirkoswald
station closed in 1970 and
reopened in 1986. The station
is in Lazonby, and Kirkoswald
is a mile away across the river.

The sidings on the right led
to the former Long Meg
mines. They produced
gypsum and anhydrite,
finally closing in 1973.
Most of the buildings have
been demolished. Long
Meg and her Daughters is a
stone circle nearby dating
back to about 4,500 BC.

LITTLE SALKELD

300 feet above sea level
Leeds 94 1/2 miles
Carlisle 18 1/2 miles

Little Salkeld station closed in
1970 and buildings remain on
the right.

LANGWATHBY

360 feet above sea level
Leeds 93 1/4 miles
Carlisle 19 3/4 miles

Langwathby station closed in
1970 and reopened in
1986.

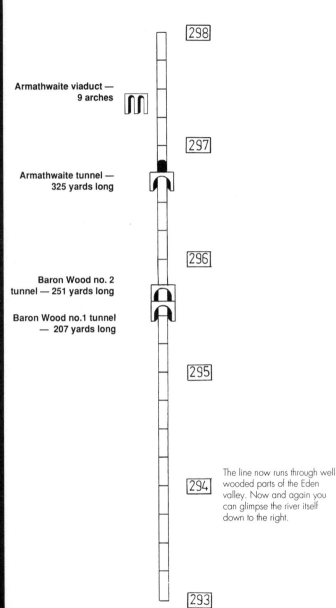

298

Armathwaite viaduct —
9 arches

297

Armathwaite tunnel —
325 yards long

296

Baron Wood no. 2
tunnel — 251 yards long

Baron Wood no.1 tunnel
— 207 yards long

295

294   The line now runs through well
wooded parts of the Eden
valley. Now and again you
can glimpse the river itself
down to the right.

293

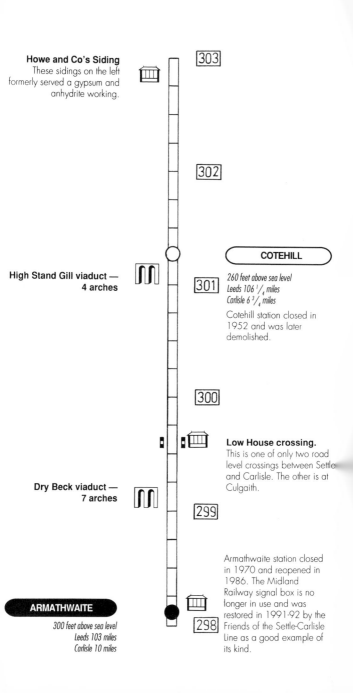

Howe and Co's Siding
These sidings on the left formerly served a gypsum and anhydrite working.

303

302

High Stand Gill viaduct — 4 arches

○

301

COTEHILL

260 feet above sea level
Leeds 106 ¼ miles
Carlisle 6 ¾ miles

Cotehill station closed in 1952 and was later demolished.

300

Low House crossing.
This is one of only two road level crossings between Settle and Carlisle. The other is at Culgaith.

Dry Beck viaduct — 7 arches

299

Armathwaite station closed in 1970 and reopened in 1986. The Midland Railway signal box is no longer in use and was restored in 1991-92 by the Friends of the Settle-Carlisle Line as a good example of its kind.

298

ARMATHWAITE

300 feet above sea level
Leeds 103 miles
Carlisle 10 miles

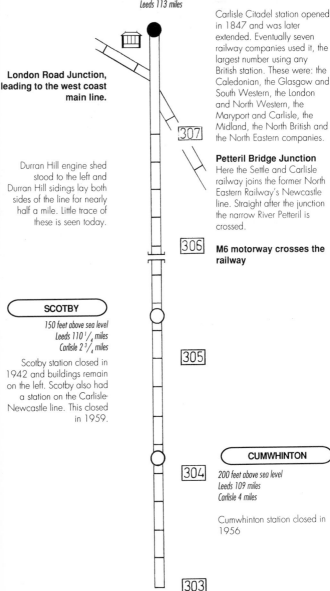

CARLISLE
70 feet above sea level
Leeds 113 miles

Carlisle Citadel station opened in 1847 and was later extended. Eventually seven railway companies used it, the largest number using any British station. These were: the Caledonian, the Glasgow and South Western, the London and North Western, the Maryport and Carlisle, the Midland, the North British and the North Eastern companies.

London Road Junction, leading to the west coast main line.

Durran Hill engine shed stood to the left and Durran Hill sidings lay both sides of the line for nearly half a mile. Little trace of these is seen today.

307

Petteril Bridge Junction
Here the Settle and Carlisle railway joins the former North Eastern Railway's Newcastle line. Straight after the junction the narrow River Petteril is crossed.

306 **M6 motorway crosses the railway**

SCOTBY
150 feet above sea level
Leeds 110 1/4 miles
Carlisle 2 3/4 miles

Scotby station closed in 1942 and buildings remain on the left. Scotby also had a station on the Carlisle-Newcastle line. This closed in 1959.

305

CUMWHINTON
200 feet above sea level
Leeds 109 miles
Carlisle 4 miles

Cumwhinton station closed in 1956

304

303

Things to see along the line

Pete Shaw

No 71000 Duke of Gloucester climbs to the summit of the line at Ais Gill

WHILE a ride on the Settle line represents an event in itself, travellers may be unaware of the many places of interest which lie along its route, many of which are only a short walk from a station.

Visitors to **Carlisle,** for example, don't have to wander far to see evidence of the city's turbulent history. The Romans built the first major fortification here and Emperor Hadrian recognised the value of *Luguvalium* when he built his famous wall from the Solway Firth to Wallsend on Tyne. The city passed from conqueror to conqueror, ravaged in turn by both the English and the Scots. The fortified city walls partially remain, but much of its stone was plundered for use in its buildings.

Carlisle cathedral is well worth a visit with its Cathedral Registry, Deanery, Fratry (monk's refectory), and Dormitory. The cathedral houses many treasures such as the Genesis Window, Dolphin's Runes, and Prior Senhouse's tomb.

Other interesting buildings include St Cuthbert's Church, Tullie House museum, Carlisle Castle museum and, for the more athletic visitor, the Sands Leisure Centre.

South of Carlisle is the small village of **Armathwaite** notable for its castle — a pele tower built for defence against raiders from the north — and the Eden Valley Woollen Mill which offers visitors a practical insight into traditional country crafts through the creation of a variety of woven fabrics.

From **Langwathby** station, you can reach Lacy's Caves. Lieutenant Colonel Samuel Lacy, who lived in Salkeld Hall in the 18th century, commissioned these five connecting chambers to be carved out of the sandstone cliff. Why he did so is unclear. The most likely explanation is that they were intended as a wine cellar, copied by Lacy from examples seen on his travels in Gibraltar.

An equally mysterious formation can be seen near Little Salkeld which is close to Langwathby station. Long Meg and her Daughters is an 18ft Neolithic standing stone overlooking 66 smaller stones arranged in an oval. Legend has it that Long Meg was a witch who conducted wild and debaucherous dances with her daughters and lover on the Sabbath, for which conduct they were turned to stone. The 300ft ellipse is claimed to be the second largest such circle in the country, after Stonehenge, and dates from about 4,500 BC.

The beautiful mediaeval town of **Appleby** offers a bustling market atmosphere and a fine Norman castle which enjoys a commanding site on a wide bend of the River Eden. The town still keeps its essentially medieval layout with the broad main street of Boroughgate leading down from the castle to the parish church. The moated grounds of the castle house a rare breed conservation centre for domestic farm animals and wildfowl. To find out more about the town visit the Tourist

Horton church with Pen-y-Ghent in the background

Information Centre which is housed in the Moot Hall at the foot of Boroughgate.

Kirkby Stephen is a handsome old market town at the northern end of the Mallerstang Valley. Granted its market charter in 1351, the town used to host many major fairs and markets and at one time boasted 17 pubs and inns. Today there is a weekly market on Mondays and regular sheep sales but churches now outnumber the pubs. Next to the cobbled market square are the cloisters where the butter market used to be held. Looking through them you can see the parish church (13th and 16th century), which is often referred to as the Cathedral of the Dales because of its size.

South of Kirkby Stephen station are the privately-owned ruins of Pendragon Castle — the legendary birthplace of King Arthur, son of Uther Pendragon. The castle is being restored under the watchful eye of English Heritage.

Hawes is a lively little town within fairly easy reach of **Ribblehead** or **Garsdale** stations, and connected to the latter by a minibus service on Tuesday (market day) and Saturday (on certain trains only). Home of the *real* Wensleydale cheese, the town also has much to recommend it to the visitor including The Dales Countryside Museum, ropemakers W R Outhwaite & Son, and many craft and gift shops, cafes and pubs.

The village of **Dent** lies four miles west of the station itself. Its ancient church, old grammar school, narrow cobbled streets and cottages, reflect the village's former importance in a community whose main source of wealth was agriculture and hand-knitting — the so-called "terrible" (very fast) knitters of Dent. The great Shap granite memorial fountain in the centre of the main street commemorates the memory of Dent-born, Adam Sedgwick — one of the greatest scientific personalities of his day and teacher to Charles Darwin. The village has many interesting craft shops, two excellent pubs and several fine cafes.

The station of **Horton in Ribblesdale** is a welcome site for exhausted ramblers as Horton is the start and end of the Three Peaks walk. This walk takes the adventurous rambler up three of the most spectacular (and wet) fells in the country — Whernside, Ingleborough, and Pen-y-Ghent. Thawing-out facilities are provided at the popular ramblers' café the Pen-y-Ghent stores (closed Tuesday). Horton also has a fine mediaeval church, village shop and a pub and lies in the middle of some of the finest caving country in England. Alum Pot, for example, about three miles north west, is one of the most spectacular potholes in the Pennines with fuming waterfalls descending a total of 300ft. Early writers imagined it as an entrance to Hell itself.

The brooding fell of Pen-y-Ghent towers over the small, grey market town of **Settle** which looks as if it has been chiselled out of the surrounding limestone countryside. The town offers a subtle blend of

HAWES

Hawes at the head of Wensleydale, is the natural centre of the Yorkshire Dales National Park and the mid-point on the Pennine Way. It is walking and rambling country, whether on high moorland, the quiet pastoral banks of the River Ure or beside impressive waterfalls.

• •

Walk the Town Trail or take your time in the Dales Countryside Museum. With shops and craft workshops, the bustling Tuesday market and livestock auctions at the mart, there is plenty to see and do. Hawes is the home of the real Wensleydale Cheese also within easy reach of the historic Settle-Carlisle railway.

Part of the fascination of watching ropes made is the satisfaction of seeing the complete process, in which many thin strands of yarn are rapidly twisted into a strong rope.

• •

Visitors are welcome to watch ropes being made. The Ropeworks is on the A684 at the entrance to Hawes Station Yard.

HOWSCALES

Cottages for non-Smokers
ETB 3/4 keys highly commended

Delightful cosy cottages set around pretty courtyard
Tranquil setting, ideal location for exploring many
local areas of interest
Colour brochure from Elaine and Colin Eade
Howscales, Kirkoswald, Penrith, Cumbria, CA10 1JG.
Tel: Lazonby (0768) 898666

the Royal Oak Inn

Bongate, Appleby-in-Westmorland, CUMBRIA CA16 6UN
Telephone: Appleby (07683) 51463

*A delightful old inn renowned for it's fresh food,
real ales and interesting wines.
The bedrooms all with private bath or
shower are very attractive.*

AA
RAC

Partners : Colin and Hilary Cheyne

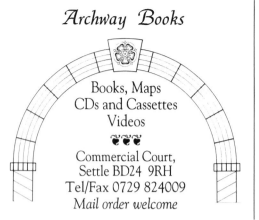

Archway Books

Books, Maps
CDs and Cassettes
Videos
🎵🎵🎵
Commercial Court,
Settle BD24 9RH
Tel/Fax 0729 824009
Mail order welcome

Jacobean, Georgian, Tudor, Victorian, and 19th century buildings interlinked by narrow lanes and well-worn cobbles. The Museum of North Craven Life, close to the town centre, offers a comprehensive insight into the town's history and gives a taste of local life and folklore. Not far from the town is the site of one of the most fascinating archaeological discoveries ever made in Britain. Victoria Cave was discovered by Michael Horner in 1838 and held many clues to its previous inhabitants including bones of bison, bear, elephant, hyena, and rhinoceros. Many of his findings are now housed in the museum.

Skipton, the 'Gateway to the Dales', is strategically situated at a crossing of the Pennines so has immense historical importance as a rail, road, and canal junction (the Leeds-Liverpool canal runs through its centre). A large and prosperous market town, it dealt in sheep and cattle before the development of its many cotton mills. The town hall houses the fascinating Craven Museum which explores Skipton's rich heritage. The town is of Norman origin, evidence of which still exists in the magnificent Skipton Castle. Built in the 14th century, the castle was a Royalist stronghold and in 1642 held out for three years against Cromwell.

Literary enthusiasts should make a point of visiting the village of Haworth near **Keighley,** home of the Brontë sisters. The museum there receives almost one million visitors a year.

The impressive village of **Saltaire** was erected by wealthy mill owner, Sir Titus Salt, for the material benefit and spiritual welfare of his massive workforce. Built between 1850 and 1860, it represents a Victorian philanthropist's vision and one which can still be seen in the village which has retained its ornate character exemplified in the great mill, with its handsome Venetian campanile-style chimney now housing an art gallery. At the peak of production the mill held 1,200 looms capable of weaving 30,000 yards of cloth every day.

Saltaire also boasts an elegant Congregational Church, a town hall — whose lions were supposed to be destined for Trafalgar Square but rejected because they were too small — and an imposing statue of Sir Titus in the riverside park. He shares his podium with two types of long-haired goat whose fleeces helped to make his fortune.

As well as being the administrative and financial centre of West Yorkshire, **Leeds** is also a major cultural centre with the West Yorkshire Playhouse, Opera North, the City Museum and Art Gallery, Kirkstall Abbey and Museum and the Henry Moore Sculpture Centre.

Much about Leeds' early history can be discovered at The Armley Mills Industrial Museum which details the city's textile and industrial heritage through the use of visual and interactive displays.

Stately homes and parks include Harewood House, Temple Newsam House, with splendid Jacobean and Tudor buildings and grounds which are host to 'Opera in the Park', the Edwardian Lotherton Hall, Roundhay Park and Tropical World which is reputed to have more visitors each year then Kew Gardens.

The city is also one of the country's major shopping areas and was the first city in the UK to introduce extensive pedestrianisation of its central streets. It has many splendid speciality shopping areas including the recently restored Corn Exchange, Granary Wharf and the Victoria Quarter which has a spectacular new stained glass roof.

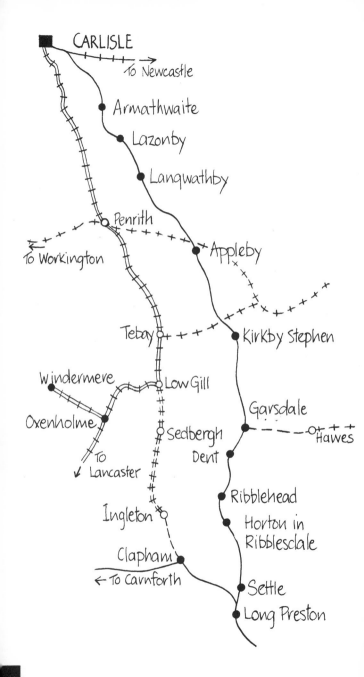

Map of the Leeds–Settle–Carlisle and associated lines showing original operating companies

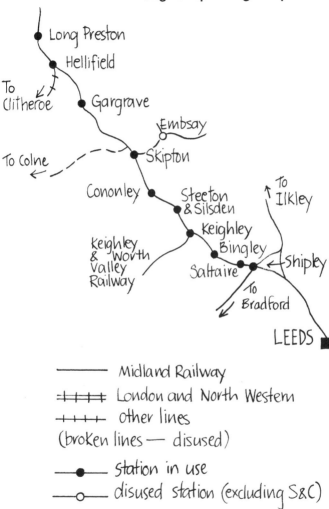

Long Preston
Hellifield
To Clitheroe
Gargrave
Embsay
Skipton
To Colne
Cononley
Steeton & Silsden
Keighley
Bingley
Keighley & Worth Valley Railway
Saltaire
To Ilkley
Shipley
To Bradford
LEEDS

———— Midland Railway
=I=I=I=I= London and North Western
+I+I+I+ other lines
(broken lines — disused)

——•—— station in use
——○—— disused station (excluding S&C)

Leeds Town Hall

LEEDS

110 feet above sea level
Carlisle 113 miles

Trains on this route originally used
Leeds Wellington station, opened in
1846 and beyond the present
platforms to the left. It was
modernised in 1938 with an
elegant concourse but is not now
used for passengers.

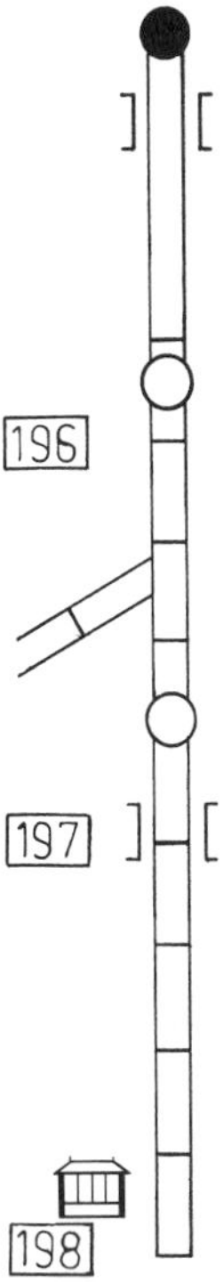

Holbeck Low Level station
closed in 1958, as did
Holbeck High Level station
above it. Nothing remains of
them today. The high level
station was on the branch to
eds Central, not far away to
he left. This was Leeds' other
ain station, closing in 1967
th rationalisation of services.

**Bridge crossing the
Leeds and Liverpool
Canal**

HOLBECK LOW LEVEL

100 feet above sea level
Carlisle 112 1/4 miles
Leeds 3/4 mile

196

Wortley Junction

from Harrogate

ridge crossing the Leeds
and Liverpool Canal

ARMLEY CANAL ROAD

110 feet above sea level
Carlisle 111 1/4 miles
Leeds 1 3/4 miles

Armley Canal Road station
closed in 1965 — buildings
remain at street level.

197

**irkstall Junction signal
box**

his was never a junction, but
the signal box served goods
lines.

198

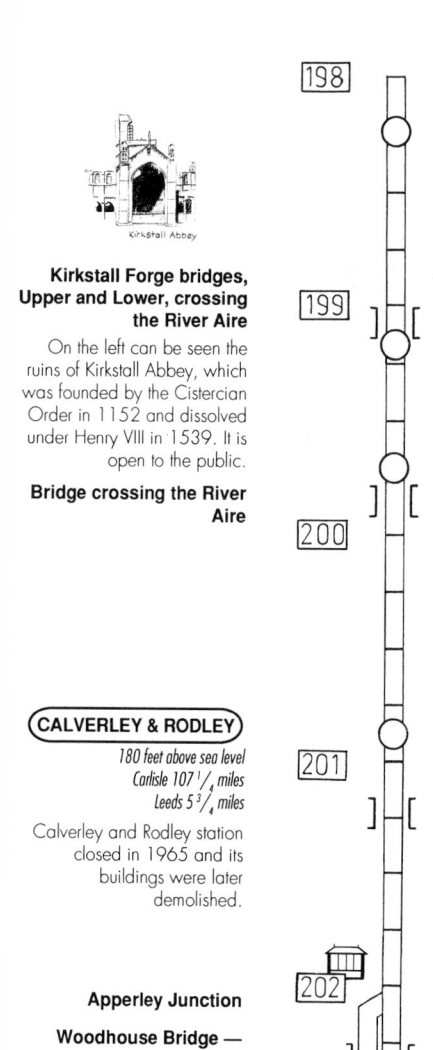

KIRKSTALL

110 feet above sea level
Carlisle 109³/₄ miles
Leeds 3¹/₄ miles

Kirkstall station closed in 19
and its buildings were later
demolished. The station wd
just before the road bridge

KIRKSTALL FORGE

150 feet above sea level
Carlisle 109 miles
Leeds 4 miles

Kirkstall Forge station closec
in 1905. It was just before
the river bridges and nothir
remains of it now.

NEWLAY

140 feet above sea level
Carlisle 108¹/₄ miles
Leeds 4³/₄ miles

Newlay station closed in
1965. It was located
immediately after the road
bridge. No buildings now
remain. Until 1961 the stati
was called Newlay and
Horsforth.

**Bridge crossing the Riv
Aire**

Apperley Bridge station clos
in 1965. It stood just after t
road bridge, but no building
are left. Till 1961 the station
was called Apperley Bridge
and Rawdon.

APPERLEY BRIDGE

200 feet above sea level
Carlisle 105¹/₂ miles
Leeds 7¹/₂ miles

Kirkstall Abbey

**Kirkstall Forge bridges,
Upper and Lower, crossing
the River Aire**

On the left can be seen the
ruins of Kirkstall Abbey, which
was founded by the Cistercian
Order in 1152 and dissolved
under Henry VIII in 1539. It is
open to the public.

**Bridge crossing the River
Aire**

CALVERLEY & RODLEY

180 feet above sea level
Carlisle 107¹/₄ miles
Leeds 5³/₄ miles

Calverley and Rodley station
closed in 1965 and its
buildings were later
demolished.

Apperley Junction

**Woodhouse Bridge —
4 arches crossing the
River Aire**

From Ilkley

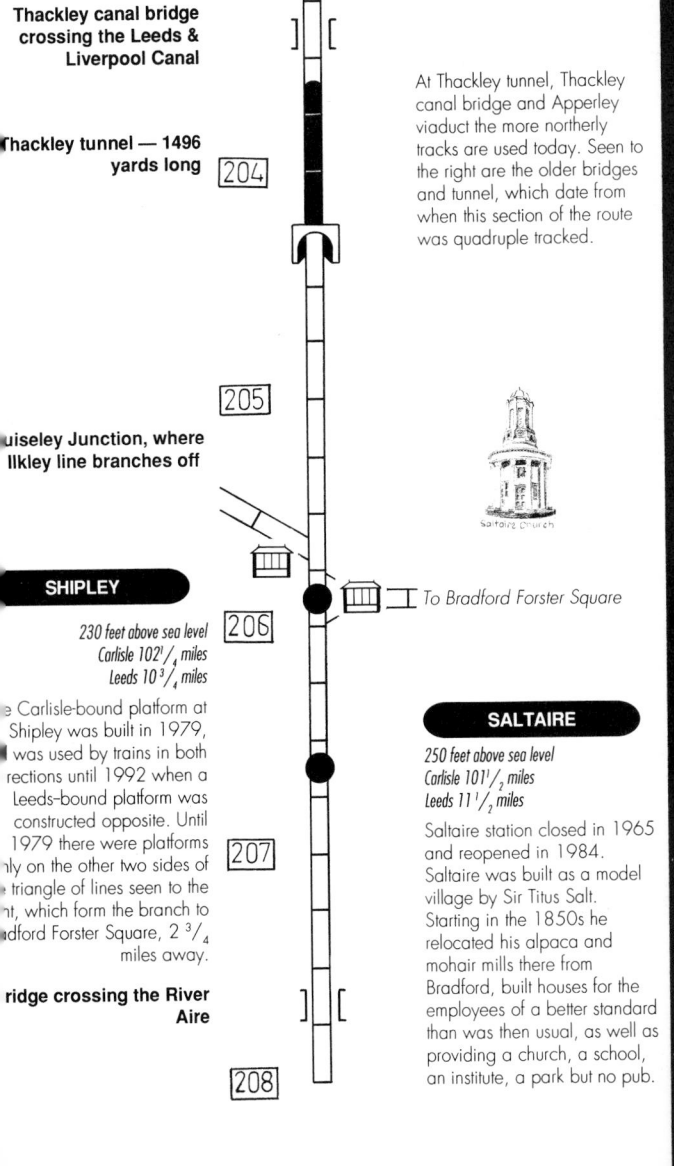

Apperley viaduct — 10 [ar]ches crossing the River Aire

`[203]`

Thackley canal bridge crossing the Leeds & Liverpool Canal

[T]hackley tunnel — 1496 yards long

`[204]`

At Thackley tunnel, Thackley canal bridge and Apperley viaduct the more northerly tracks are used today. Seen to the right are the older bridges and tunnel, which date from when this section of the route was quadruple tracked.

`[205]`

[Q]uiseley Junction, where [I]lkley line branches off

Saltaire Church

SHIPLEY

230 feet above sea level
Carlisle 102¹/₄ miles
Leeds 10³/₄ miles

`[206]`

━━▶ *To Bradford Forster Square*

[Th]e Carlisle-bound platform at Shipley was built in 1979, [an]d was used by trains in both [di]rections until 1992 when a Leeds-bound platform was constructed opposite. Until 1979 there were platforms [on]ly on the other two sides of [the] triangle of lines seen to the [rig]ht, which form the branch to [Bra]dford Forster Square, 2 ³/₄ miles away.

`[207]`

SALTAIRE

250 feet above sea level
Carlisle 101¹/₂ miles
Leeds 11¹/₂ miles

Saltaire station closed in 1965 and reopened in 1984. Saltaire was built as a model village by Sir Titus Salt. Starting in the 1850s he relocated his alpaca and mohair mills there from Bradford, built houses for the employees of a better standard than was then usual, as well as providing a church, a school, an institute, a park but no pub.

[b]ridge crossing the River Aire

`[208]`

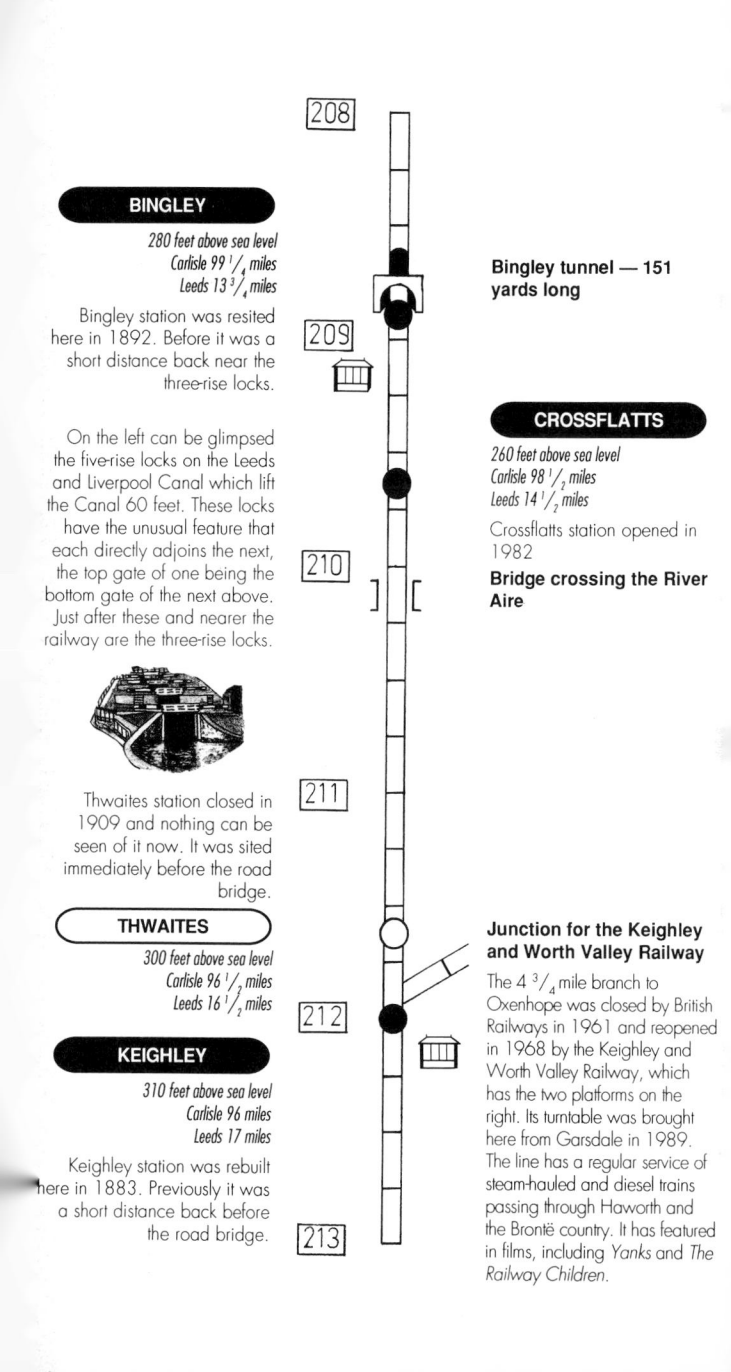

208

BINGLEY

280 feet above sea level
Carlisle 99 1/4 miles
Leeds 13 3/4 miles

Bingley station was resited here in 1892. Before it was a short distance back near the three-rise locks.

On the left can be glimpsed the five-rise locks on the Leeds and Liverpool Canal which lift the Canal 60 feet. These locks have the unusual feature that each directly adjoins the next, the top gate of one being the bottom gate of the next above. Just after these and nearer the railway are the three-rise locks.

Thwaites station closed in 1909 and nothing can be seen of it now. It was sited immediately before the road bridge.

THWAITES

300 feet above sea level
Carlisle 96 1/4 miles
Leeds 16 1/2 miles

KEIGHLEY

310 feet above sea level
Carlisle 96 miles
Leeds 17 miles

Keighley station was rebuilt here in 1883. Previously it was a short distance back before the road bridge.

209

210

211

212

213

Bingley tunnel — 151 yards long

CROSSFLATTS

260 feet above sea level
Carlisle 98 1/2 miles
Leeds 14 1/2 miles

Crossflatts station opened in 1982

Bridge crossing the River Aire

Junction for the Keighley and Worth Valley Railway

The 4 3/4 mile branch to Oxenhope was closed by British Railways in 1961 and reopened in 1968 by the Keighley and Worth Valley Railway, which has the two platforms on the right. Its turntable was brought here from Garsdale in 1989. The line has a regular service of steam-hauled and diesel trains passing through Haworth and the Brontë country. It has featured in films, including *Yanks* and *The Railway Children*.

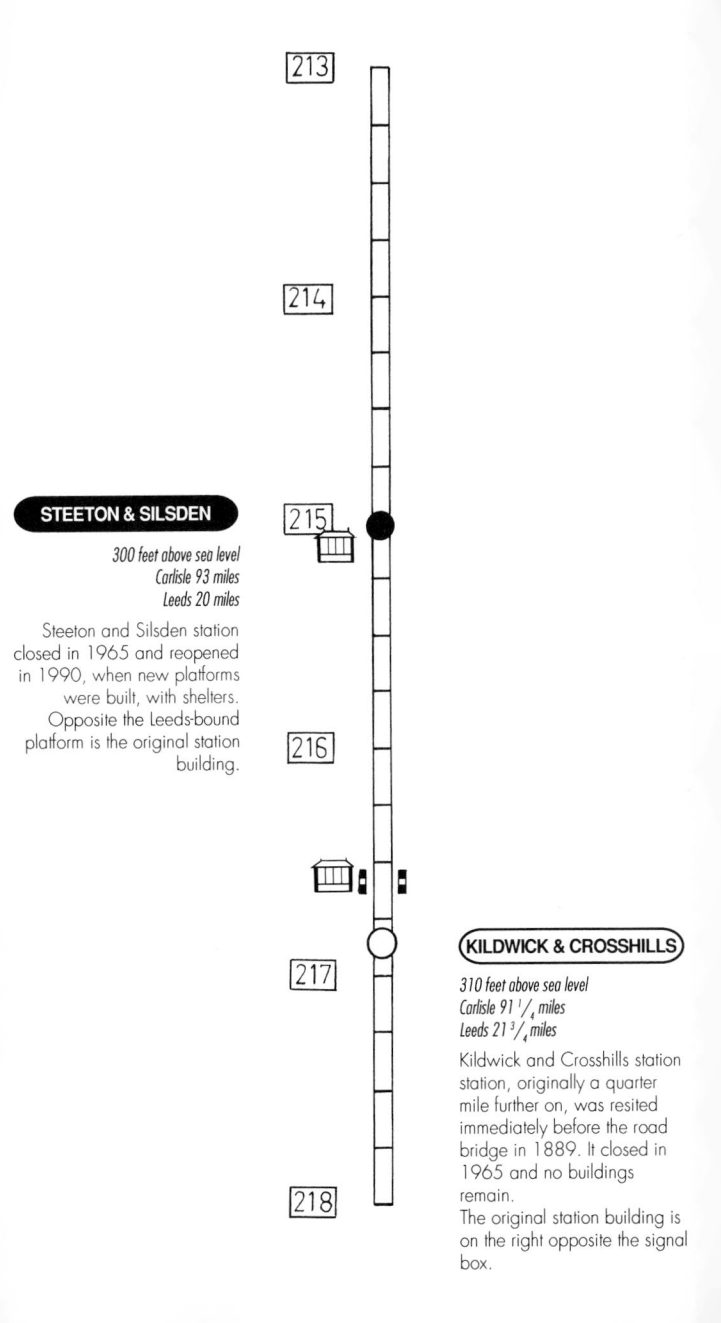

213

214

STEETON & SILSDEN

300 feet above sea level
Carlisle 93 miles
Leeds 20 miles

Steeton and Silsden station
closed in 1965 and reopened
in 1990, when new platforms
were built, with shelters.
Opposite the Leeds-bound
platform is the original station
building.

215

216

KILDWICK & CROSSHILLS

310 feet above sea level
Carlisle 91 $\frac{1}{4}$ miles
Leeds 21 $\frac{3}{4}$ miles

Kildwick and Crosshills station
station, originally a quarter
mile further on, was resited
immediately before the road
bridge in 1889. It closed in
1965 and no buildings
remain.
The original station building is
on the right opposite the signal
box.

217

218

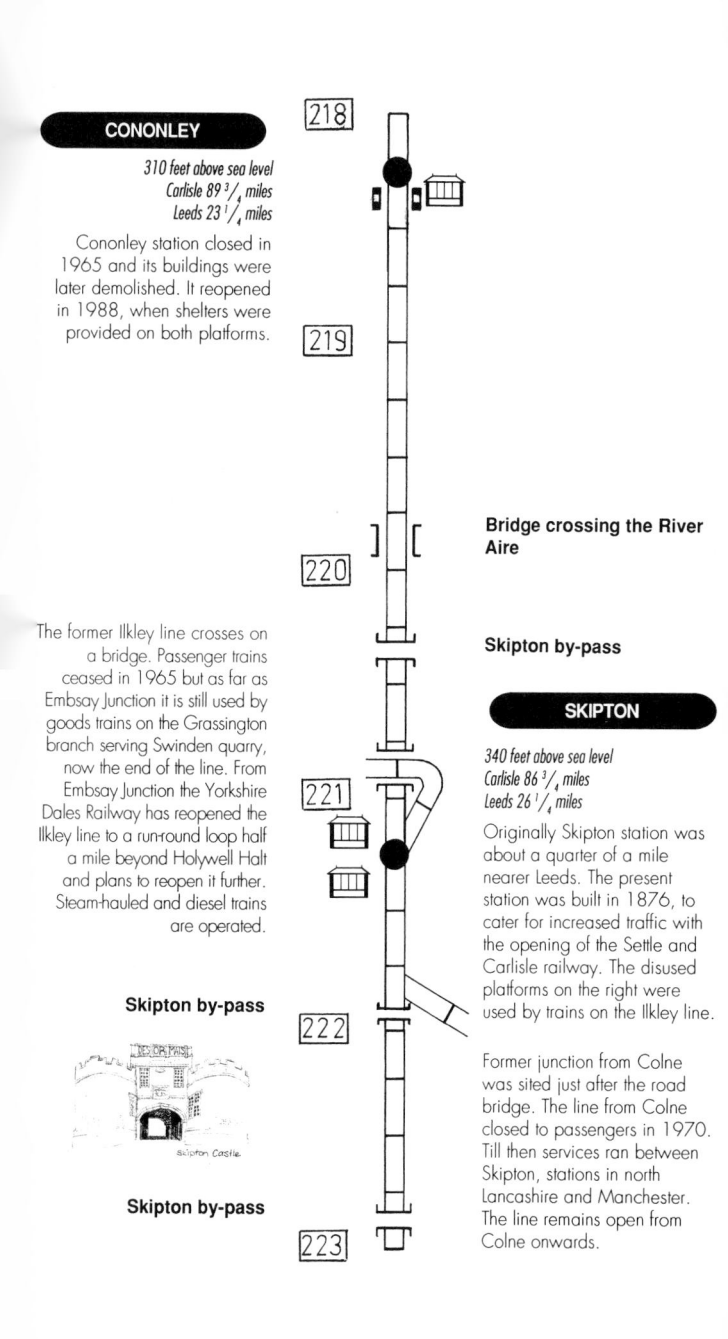

CONONLEY

310 feet above sea level
Carlisle 89 ³/₄ miles
Leeds 23 ¹/₄ miles

Cononley station closed in 1965 and its buildings were later demolished. It reopened in 1988, when shelters were provided on both platforms.

The former Ilkley line crosses on a bridge. Passenger trains ceased in 1965 but as far as Embsay Junction it is still used by goods trains on the Grassington branch serving Swinden quarry, now the end of the line. From Embsay Junction the Yorkshire Dales Railway has reopened the Ilkley line to a run-round loop half a mile beyond Holywell Halt and plans to reopen it further. Steam-hauled and diesel trains are operated.

Skipton by-pass

Skipton Castle

Skipton by-pass

Bridge crossing the River Aire

Skipton by-pass

SKIPTON

340 feet above sea level
Carlisle 86 ³/₄ miles
Leeds 26 ¹/₄ miles

Originally Skipton station was about a quarter of a mile nearer Leeds. The present station was built in 1876, to cater for increased traffic with the opening of the Settle and Carlisle railway. The disused platforms on the right were used by trains on the Ilkley line.

Former junction from Colne was sited just after the road bridge. The line from Colne closed to passengers in 1970. Till then services ran between Skipton, stations in north Lancashire and Manchester. The line remains open from Colne onwards.

218 219 220 221 222 223

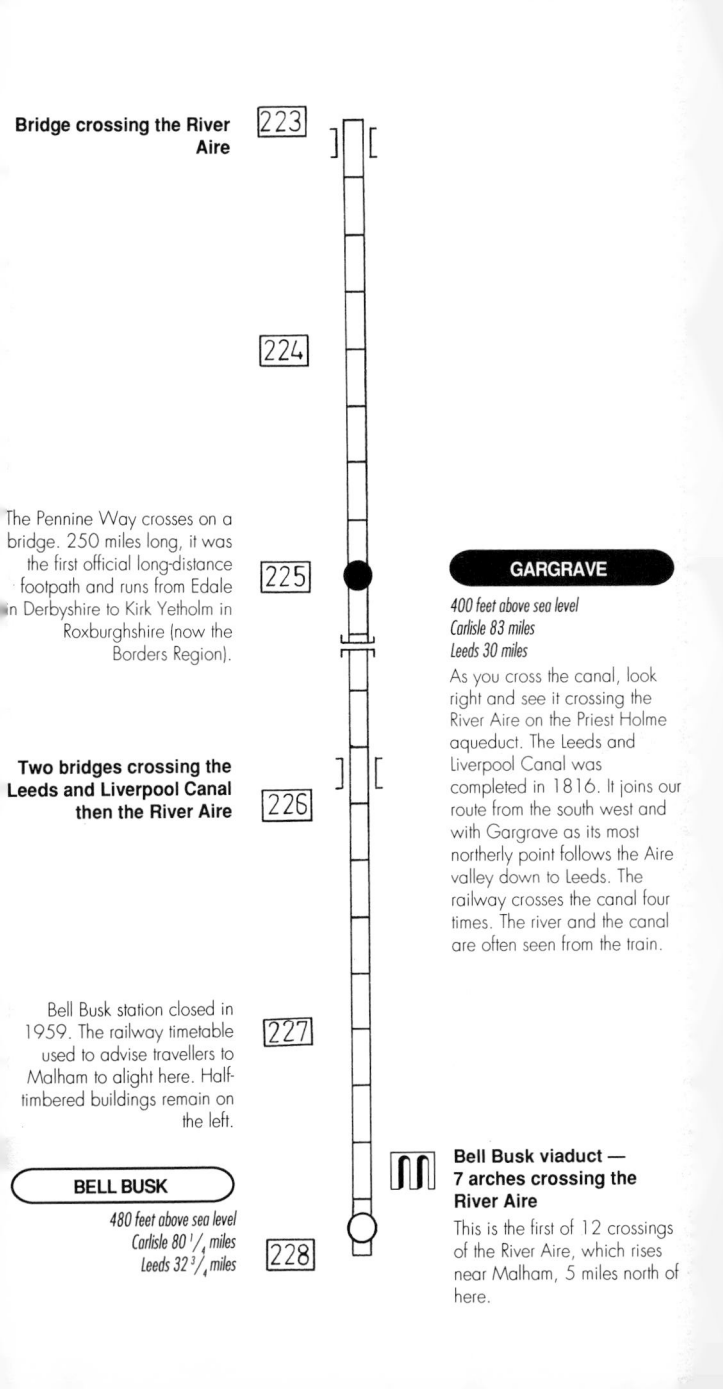

Bridge crossing the River Aire | 223

The Pennine Way crosses on a bridge. 250 miles long, it was the first official long-distance footpath and runs from Edale in Derbyshire to Kirk Yetholm in Roxburghshire (now the Borders Region). | 225

GARGRAVE

400 feet above sea level
Carlisle 83 miles
Leeds 30 miles

As you cross the canal, look right and see it crossing the River Aire on the Priest Holme aqueduct. The Leeds and Liverpool Canal was completed in 1816. It joins our route from the south west and with Gargrave as its most northerly point follows the Aire valley down to Leeds. The railway crosses the canal four times. The river and the canal are often seen from the train.

Two bridges crossing the Leeds and Liverpool Canal then the River Aire | 226

Bell Busk station closed in 1959. The railway timetable used to advise travellers to Malham to alight here. Half-timbered buildings remain on the left. | 227

BELL BUSK

480 feet above sea level
Carlisle 80 1/4 miles
Leeds 32 3/4 miles

228

Bell Busk viaduct — 7 arches crossing the River Aire

This is the first of 12 crossings of the River Aire, which rises near Malham, 5 miles north of here.

Hellifeld South Junction is the s[...]
of the Lancashire & Yorkshire
Railway line opened in 1880[...]
closed to regular passenger
services in 1962, staying ope[...]
for goods traffic, and diversion[...]
when the west coast main line[...]
closed between Carlisle and
Preston. On such occasions tr[...]
go from Carlisle to Settle and
Hellifield then via Blackburn to[...]
Preston. The first stage of
reopening was in 1990, whe[...]
summer Saturday services beg[...]
between Blackburn and
Clitheroe. Soon, it is hoped, t[...]
whole line from Hellifield to
Blackburn will be open,
providing, as in times past, tra[...]
and connections between
Manchester and towns in nort[...]
Lancashire and the Settle and
Carlisle railway.
For details of the campaign to[...]
promote the Blackburn-Hellifie[...]
line see page 12.

228

229

Down from Ribblehead the
railway has followed the
Ribble valley. Here it passes
gently over the watershed to
the Aire valley, which it follows
the whole way to Leeds.

230

To Clitheroe and Blackburn

HELLIFIELD

520 feet above sea level
Carlisle 76 $\frac{3}{4}$ miles
Leeds 36 $\frac{1}{4}$ miles
The present Hellifield station
building dates from 1880. It is
a Grade 2 listed building, with
the longest Midland Railway
canopy still in existence. Its
decorative ironwork
incorporates the company's
initials and heraldic wyverns
which watched over the
junction in its departed glorious
days, when it was busy with
passengers and employees.
Many expresses and local trains
called here and there were two
engine sheds.
Today Hellifield is unstaffed and
part of the platforms cannot be
used. The station's future has not
yet been decided.

231

232

Over to the right is the long
shape of Pendle Hill, 1831
feet high, and 10 miles aw[...]

LONG PRESTON

460 feet above sea level
Carlisle 75 $\frac{1}{2}$ miles
Leeds 37 $\frac{1}{2}$ miles

233

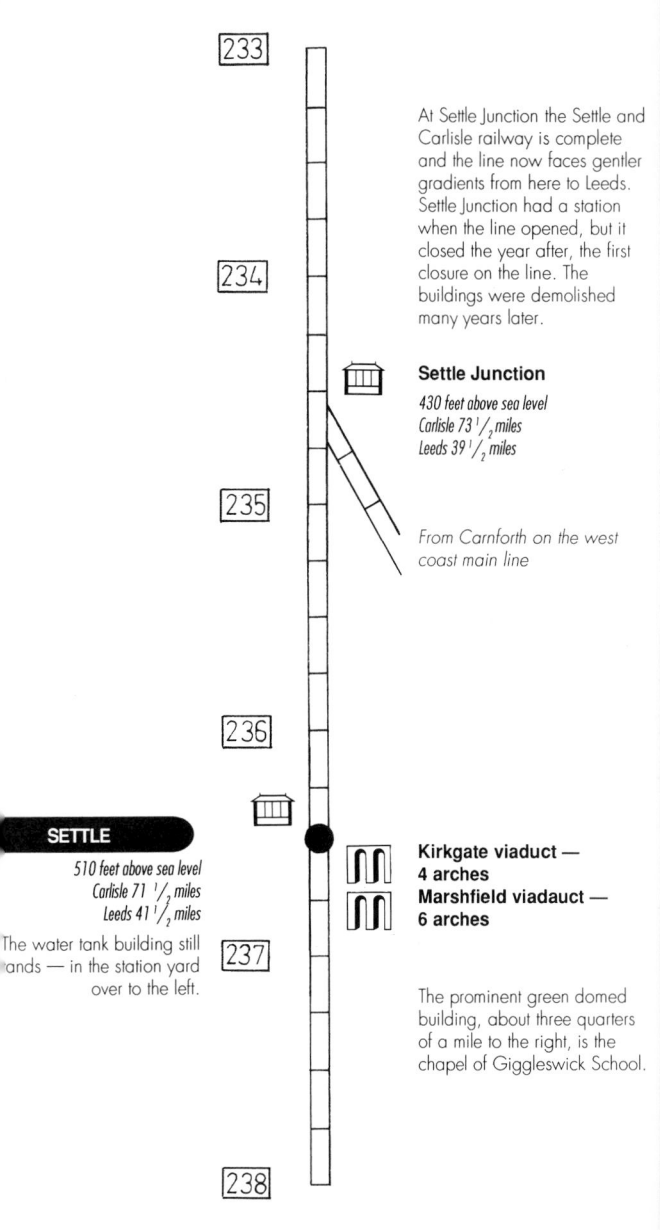

233

234

At Settle Junction the Settle and Carlisle railway is complete and the line now faces gentler gradients from here to Leeds. Settle Junction had a station when the line opened, but it closed the year after, the first closure on the line. The buildings were demolished many years later.

Settle Junction
430 feet above sea level
Carlisle 73 ¹/₂ miles
Leeds 39 ¹/₂ miles

From Carnforth on the west coast main line

235

236

SETTLE
510 feet above sea level
Carlisle 71 ¹/₂ miles
Leeds 41 ¹/₂ miles

The water tank building still stands — in the station yard over to the left.

237

**Kirkgate viaduct —
4 arches
Marshfield viadauct —
6 arches**

The prominent green domed building, about three quarters of a mile to the right, is the chapel of Giggleswick School.

238

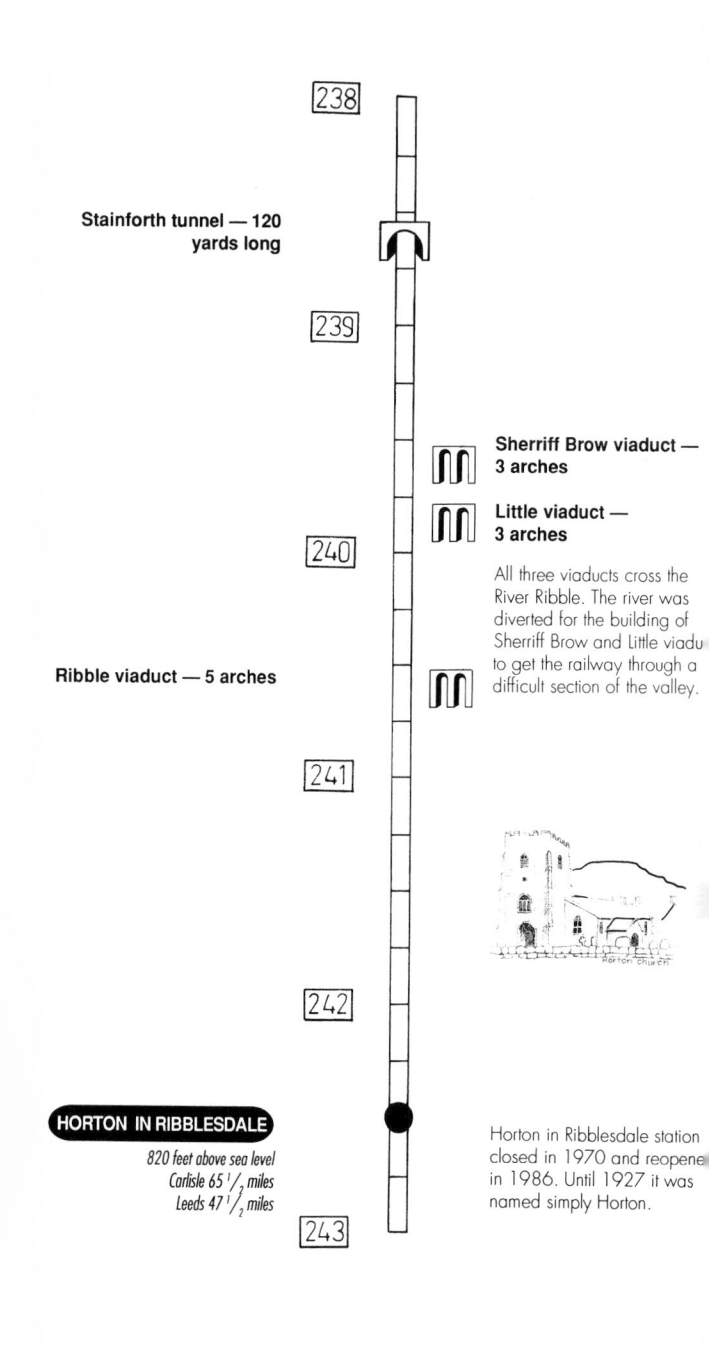

Stainforth tunnel — 120 yards long

238

239

Sherriff Brow viaduct — 3 arches

Little viaduct — 3 arches

All three viaducts cross the River Ribble. The river was diverted for the building of Sherriff Brow and Little viadu to get the railway through a difficult section of the valley.

240

Ribble viaduct — 5 arches

241

242

HORTON IN RIBBLESDALE

820 feet above sea level
Carlisle 65 ¹/₂ miles
Leeds 47 ¹/₂ miles

243

Horton in Ribblesdale station closed in 1970 and reopene in 1986. Until 1927 it was named simply Horton.

243

244

...minent to the left in this area
...Pen-y-Ghent, 3 miles away
and 2272 feet high.

...estone quarries and lime
...rkings are a feature of the
...ble valley down nearly as
...as Settle.

245

...ring the railway construction
...riod shanty towns were built
for the workforce and their
...amilies. Some of these were
around Blea Moor tunnel,
...low Ribblehead viaduct and
...yond, but little trace remains
...them today. A tramway was
built from the road at
...ibblehead to carry materials
...or the building of Blea Moor
tunnel, and parts of its
trackbed can still be seen.

Ribblehead station closed in
1970 and reopened in 1986
for southbound trains only. The
northbound platform had been
removed when a branch for
the quarry on the right was
built. A new northbound
platform opened in summer
1993. The station in times past
has been a centre for the local
scattered community and a
reporting point for
meteorological data. The
stationmaster regularly sent in
details such as rainfall and
windspeed.

246

Ribblehead viaduct

Ribblehead is by far the
longest viaduct on the route,
taking the railway from the
mountainous section to run
down the Ribble valley. In
1985 nearly a mile of track
was singled to reduce wear
and tear on the viaduct.

247

RIBBLEHEAD

1030 feet above sea level
Carlisle 60 $\frac{3}{4}$ miles
Leeds 52 $\frac{1}{4}$ miles

Single track section ends

**Ribblehead viaduct —
24 arches**

248

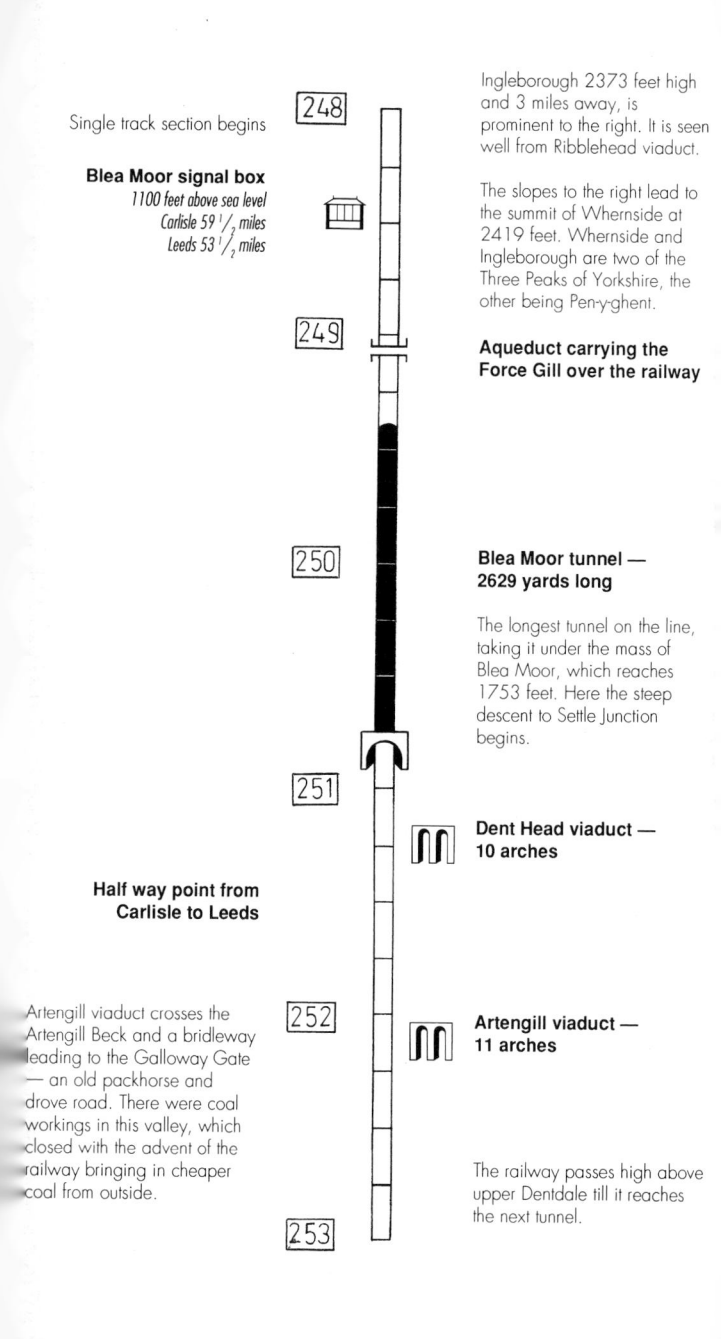

Single track section begins

Blea Moor signal box
1100 feet above sea level
Carlisle 59 1/2 miles
Leeds 53 1/2 miles

248

249

250

251

**Half way point from
Carlisle to Leeds**

252

Artengill viaduct crosses the
Artengill Beck and a bridleway
leading to the Galloway Gate
— an old packhorse and
drove road. There were coal
workings in this valley, which
closed with the advent of the
railway bringing in cheaper
coal from outside.

253

Ingleborough 2373 feet high
and 3 miles away, is
prominent to the right. It is seen
well from Ribblehead viaduct.

The slopes to the right lead to
the summit of Whernside at
2419 feet. Whernside and
Ingleborough are two of the
Three Peaks of Yorkshire, the
other being Pen-y-ghent.

**Aqueduct carrying the
Force Gill over the railway**

**Blea Moor tunnel —
2629 yards long**

The longest tunnel on the line,
taking it under the mass of
Blea Moor, which reaches
1753 feet. Here the steep
descent to Settle Junction
begins.

**Dent Head viaduct —
10 arches**

**Artengill viaduct —
11 arches**

The railway passes high above
upper Dentdale till it reaches
the next tunnel.

DENT

1150 feet above sea level
Carlisle 54 3/4 miles
Leeds 58 1/4 miles

Dent station closed in 1970 and reopened in 1986. Dent itself is some 4 miles to the left and over 600 feet lower. Dent station is England's highest. Higher ones, like Princetown in Devon at 1373 feet, have all closed.

Garsdale water troughs *(at milepost 256)* now removed, were the highest in Britain. A trough between each pair of rails allowed steam engines to take water up at speed. Over a quarter of a mile long, they were fed from a tank on the left and were once steam-heated.

Former junction for Hawes. The Wensleydale Railway, the only branch constructed on the Settle and Carlisle railway, opened two years after the main line in 1878. Its 6 miles of single track closed in 1959. Beyond Hawes the North Eastern Railway continued the line down Wensleydale to Northallerton on the east coast main line and this section closed to passenger trains in 1954. For prospects of reopening see page 12.

Moorcock tunnel —
98 yards long

Soon after Moorcock tunnel there is a glimpse of upper Wensleydale to the left, then the line passes high up along Garsdale.

Between Rise Hill tunnel and Dent Head viaduct the remains of snow fences stand on the left high above the railway, bearing witness to the severe winters of past years. Snow in fact blocked the line for two months in 1947 despite many efforts to clear it. In 1963 again it was blocked, though this time relatively briefly.

Emerging from Rise Hill tunnel, the line goes at high level round the head of Dentdale, the valley down to the right, till it plunges into the next tunnel.

Rise Hill tunnel —
1213 yards long

The river on the right is the Clough River, with the slopes of Baugh Fell (summit 2216 feet) beyond it.

Originally called Hawes Junction, Garsdale station closed in 1970 and reopened in 1986. In the heyday of steam, pilot engines which had assisted trains up the gradients from north and south were detached at Garsdale, turned and then they returned home. The turntable was removed to the Keighley and Worth Valley Railway in 1989, where it has been restored to use.

GARSDALE

1130 feet above sea level
Carlisle 51 1/2 miles
Leeds 61 1/2 miles

Dandry Mire viaduct —
12 arches

An embankment was planned here but ground conditions proved unsuitable, so Dandry Mire viaduct was built instead

Lunds viaduct — 5 arches

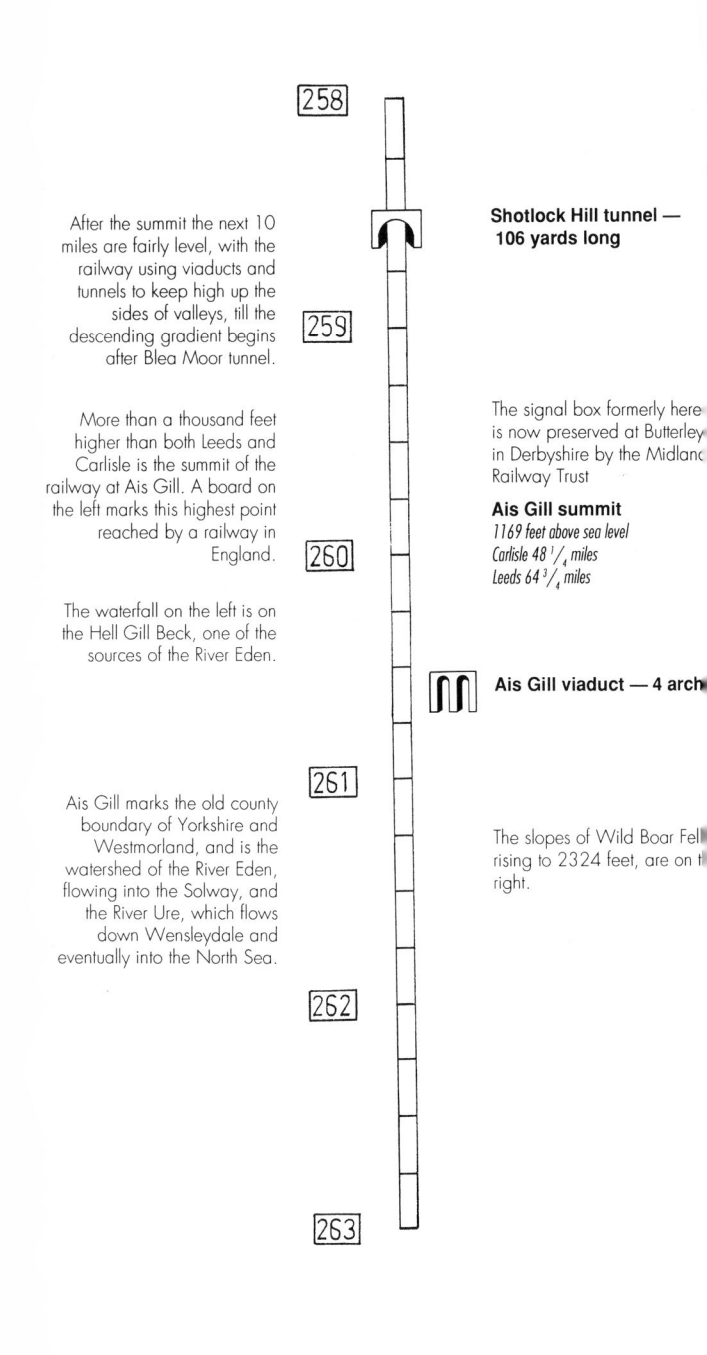

258

After the summit the next 10 miles are fairly level, with the railway using viaducts and tunnels to keep high up the sides of valleys, till the descending gradient begins after Blea Moor tunnel.

Shotlock Hill tunnel — 106 yards long

259

More than a thousand feet higher than both Leeds and Carlisle is the summit of the railway at Ais Gill. A board on the left marks this highest point reached by a railway in England.

The signal box formerly here is now preserved at Butterley in Derbyshire by the Midland Railway Trust

Ais Gill summit
1169 feet above sea level
Carlisle 48 ¹/₄ miles
Leeds 64 ³/₄ miles

The waterfall on the left is on the Hell Gill Beck, one of the sources of the River Eden.

260

Ais Gill viaduct — 4 arch

261

Ais Gill marks the old county boundary of Yorkshire and Westmorland, and is the watershed of the River Eden, flowing into the Solway, and the River Ure, which flows down Wensleydale and eventually into the North Sea.

The slopes of Wild Boar Fell rising to 2324 feet, are on the right.

262

263

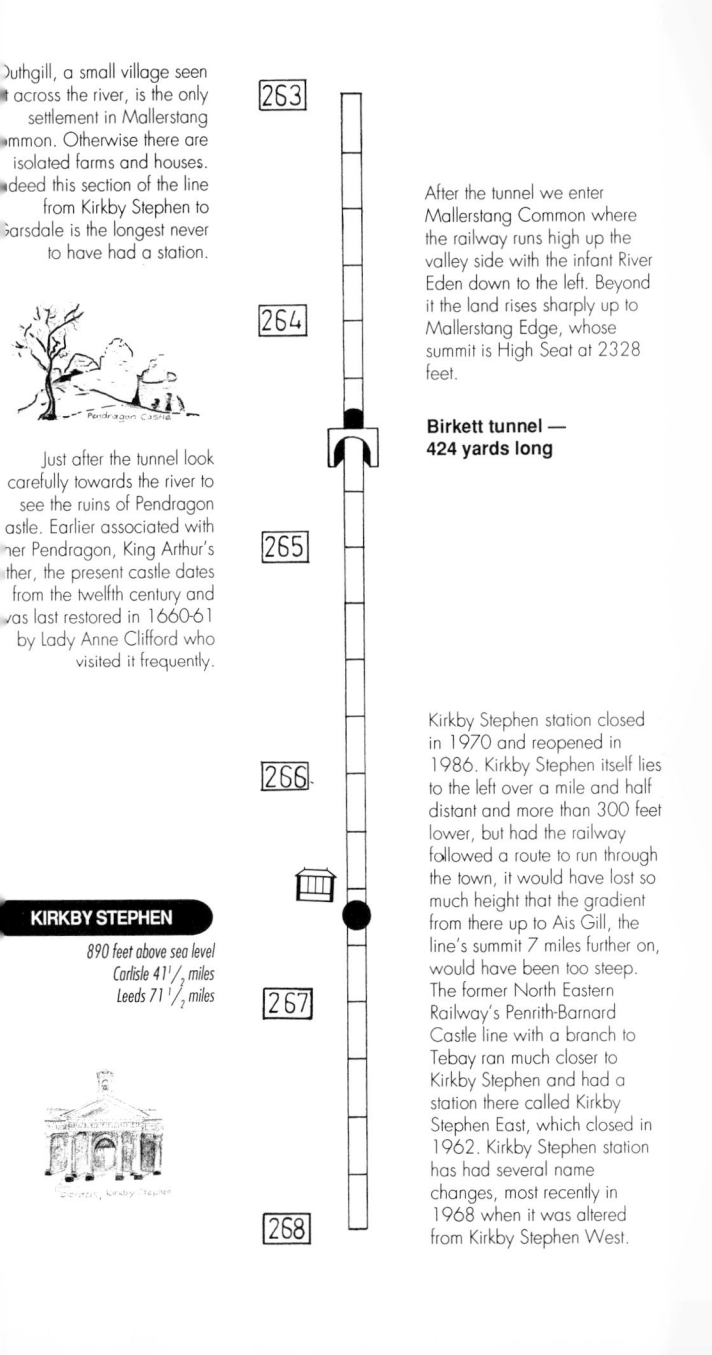

Outhgill, a small village seen across the river, is the only settlement in Mallerstang Common. Otherwise there are isolated farms and houses. Indeed this section of the line from Kirkby Stephen to Garsdale is the longest never to have had a station.

Just after the tunnel look carefully towards the river to see the ruins of Pendragon Castle. Earlier associated with Uther Pendragon, King Arthur's father, the present castle dates from the twelfth century and was last restored in 1660-61 by Lady Anne Clifford who visited it frequently.

263

264

265

266

267

268

After the tunnel we enter Mallerstang Common where the railway runs high up the valley side with the infant River Eden down to the left. Beyond it the land rises sharply up to Mallerstang Edge, whose summit is High Seat at 2328 feet.

**Birkett tunnel —
424 yards long**

Kirkby Stephen station closed in 1970 and reopened in 1986. Kirkby Stephen itself lies to the left over a mile and half distant and more than 300 feet lower, but had the railway followed a route to run through the town, it would have lost so much height that the gradient from there up to Ais Gill, the line's summit 7 miles further on, would have been too steep. The former North Eastern Railway's Penrith-Barnard Castle line with a branch to Tebay ran much closer to Kirkby Stephen and had a station there called Kirkby Stephen East, which closed in 1962. Kirkby Stephen station has had several name changes, most recently in 1968 when it was altered from Kirkby Stephen West.

KIRKBY STEPHEN

890 feet above sea level
Carlisle 41$\frac{1}{2}$ miles
Leeds 71$\frac{1}{2}$ miles

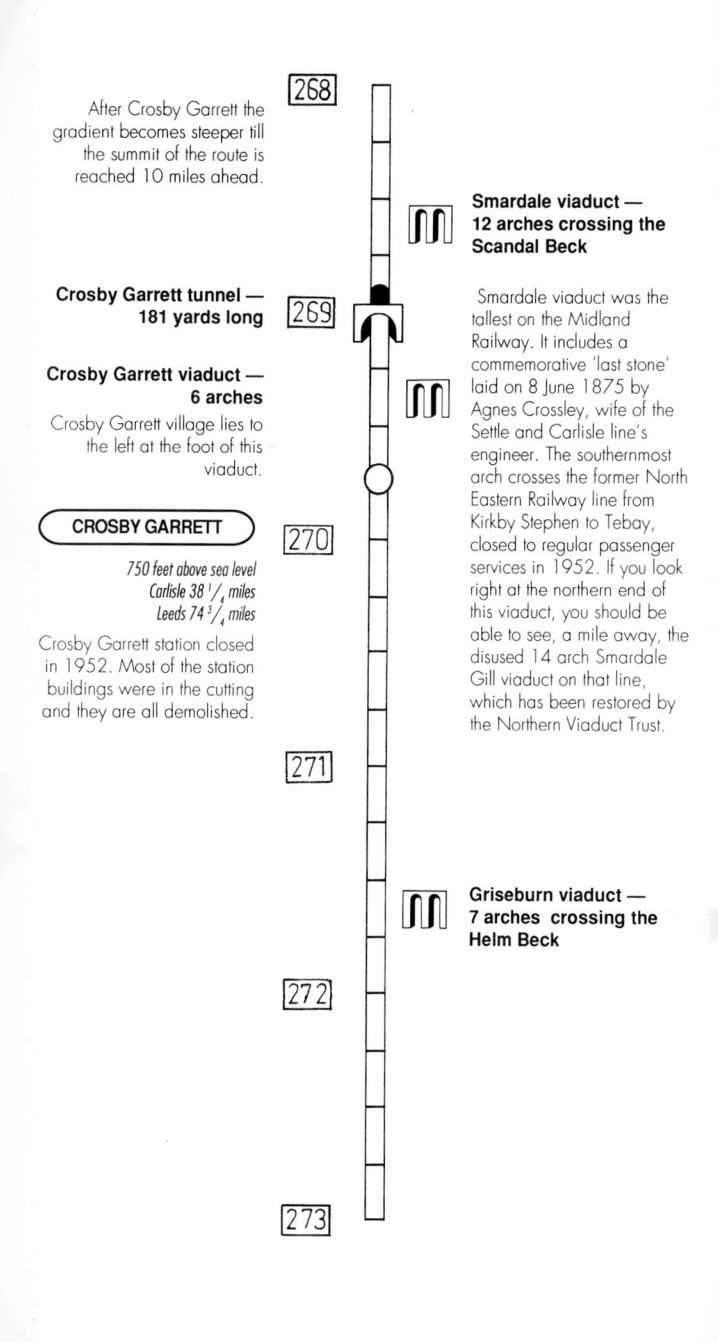

After Crosby Garrett the gradient becomes steeper till the summit of the route is reached 10 miles ahead.

268

**Smardale viaduct —
12 arches crossing the
Scandal Beck**

Smardale viaduct was the tallest on the Midland Railway. It includes a commemorative 'last stone' laid on 8 June 1875 by Agnes Crossley, wife of the Settle and Carlisle line's engineer. The southernmost arch crosses the former North Eastern Railway line from Kirkby Stephen to Tebay, closed to regular passenger services in 1952. If you look right at the northern end of this viaduct, you should be able to see, a mile away, the disused 14 arch Smardale Gill viaduct on that line, which has been restored by the Northern Viaduct Trust.

**Crosby Garrett tunnel —
181 yards long**

269

**Crosby Garrett viaduct —
6 arches**

Crosby Garrett village lies to the left at the foot of this viaduct.

CROSBY GARRETT

750 feet above sea level
Carlisle 38 1/4 miles
Leeds 74 3/4 miles

Crosby Garrett station closed in 1952. Most of the station buildings were in the cutting and they are all demolished.

270

271

**Griseburn viaduct —
7 arches crossing the
Helm Beck**

272

273

Helm tunnel — 571 yards long

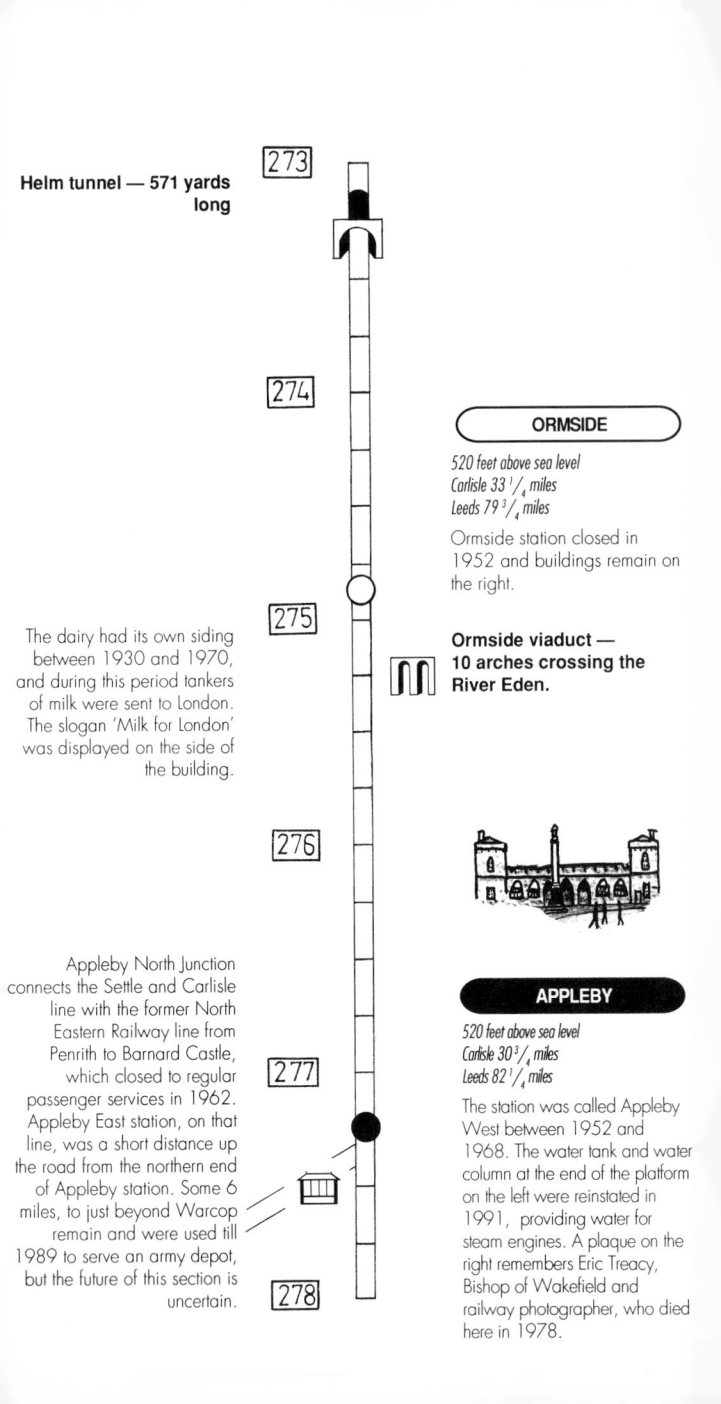

273

274

ORMSIDE

520 feet above sea level
Carlisle 33 1/4 miles
Leeds 79 3/4 miles

Ormside station closed in 1952 and buildings remain on the right.

275

The dairy had its own siding between 1930 and 1970, and during this period tankers of milk were sent to London. The slogan 'Milk for London' was displayed on the side of the building.

Ormside viaduct — 10 arches crossing the River Eden.

276

APPLEBY

520 feet above sea level
Carlisle 30 3/4 miles
Leeds 82 1/4 miles

The station was called Appleby West between 1952 and 1968. The water tank and water column at the end of the platform on the left were reinstated in 1991, providing water for steam engines. A plaque on the right remembers Eric Treacy, Bishop of Wakefield and railway photographer, who died here in 1978.

277

Appleby North Junction connects the Settle and Carlisle line with the former North Eastern Railway line from Penrith to Barnard Castle, which closed to regular passenger services in 1962. Appleby East station, on that line, was a short distance up the road from the northern end of Appleby station. Some 6 miles, to just beyond Warcop remain and were used till 1989 to serve an army depot, but the future of this section is uncertain.

278

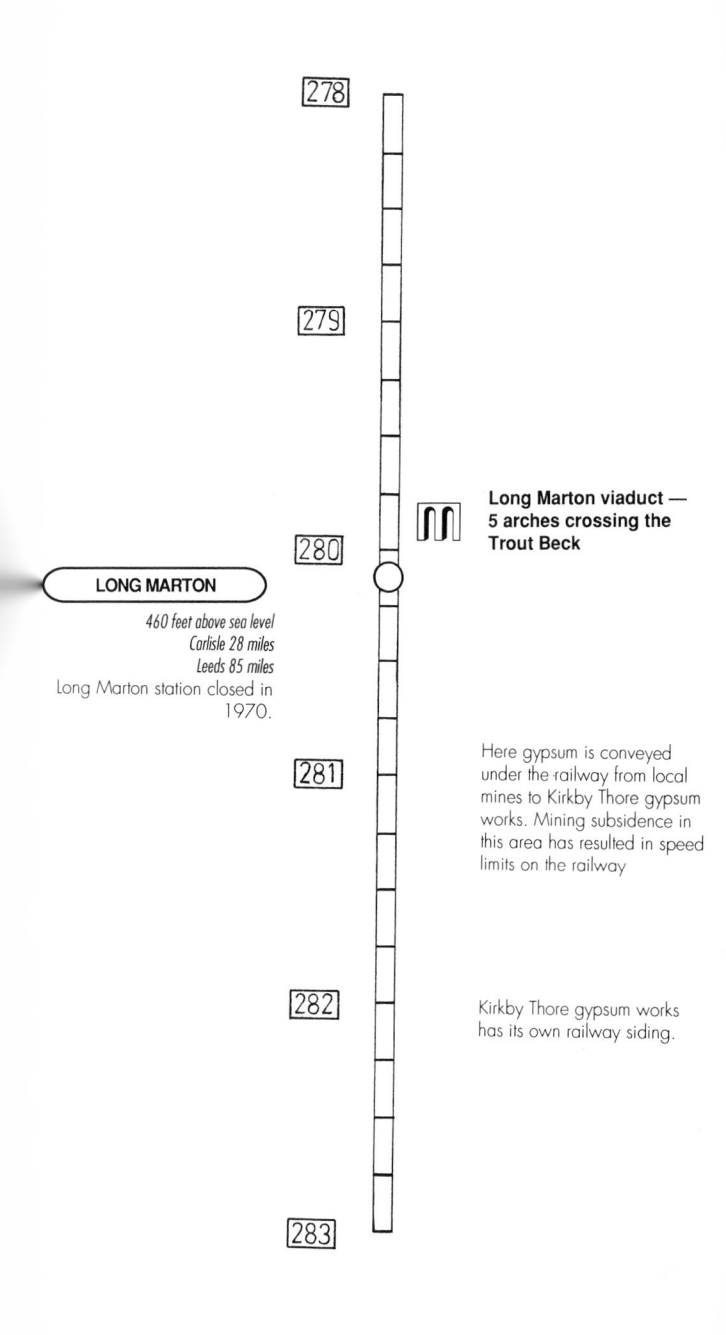

278

279

**Long Marton viaduct —
5 arches crossing the
Trout Beck**

280

LONG MARTON

460 feet above sea level
Carlisle 28 miles
Leeds 85 miles
Long Marton station closed in
1970.

281

Here gypsum is conveyed
under the railway from local
mines to Kirkby Thore gypsum
works. Mining subsidence in
this area has resulted in speed
limits on the railway

282

Kirkby Thore gypsum works
has its own railway siding.

283

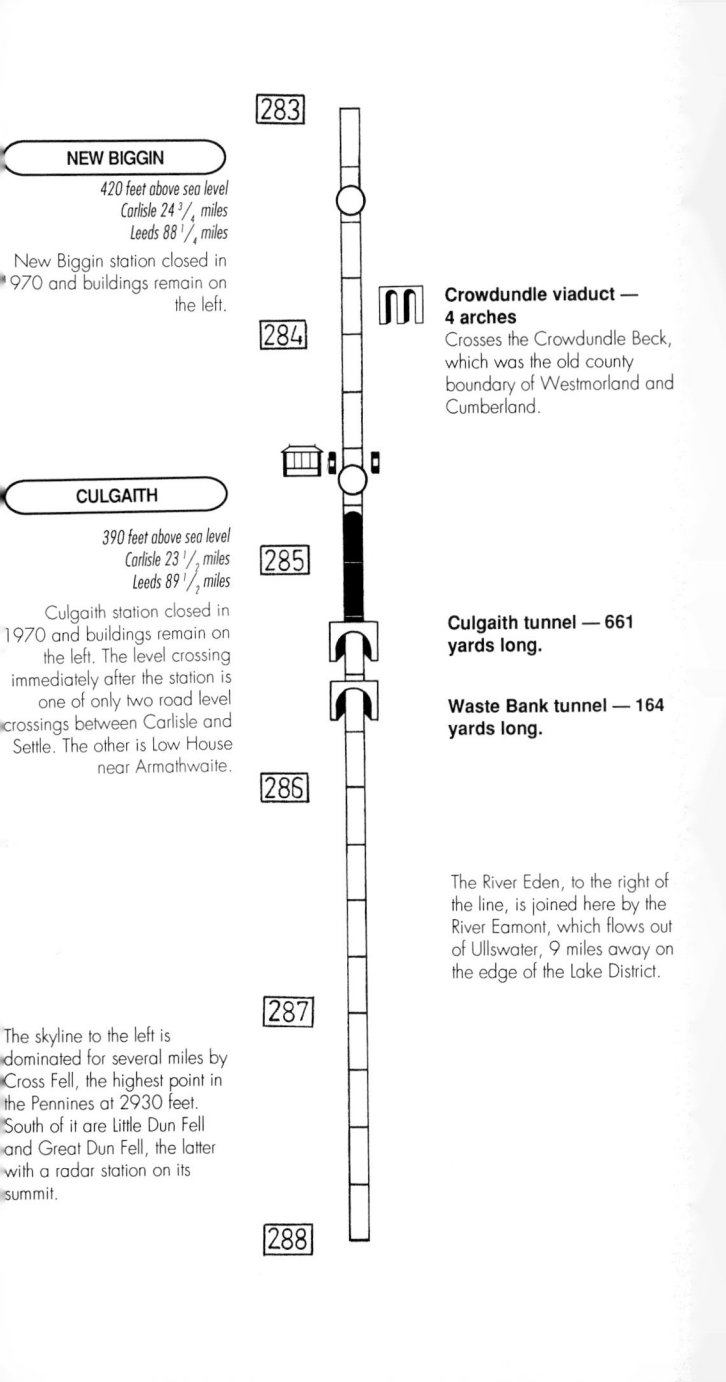

283

NEW BIGGIN

420 feet above sea level
Carlisle 24 ³/₄ miles
Leeds 88 ¹/₄ miles

New Biggin station closed in
1970 and buildings remain on
the left.

284

**Crowdundle viaduct —
4 arches**
Crosses the Crowdundle Beck,
which was the old county
boundary of Westmorland and
Cumberland.

CULGAITH

390 feet above sea level
Carlisle 23 ¹/₂ miles
Leeds 89 ¹/₂ miles

285

Culgaith station closed in
1970 and buildings remain on
the left. The level crossing
immediately after the station is
one of only two road level
crossings between Carlisle and
Settle. The other is Low House
near Armathwaite.

**Culgaith tunnel — 661
yards long.**

**Waste Bank tunnel — 164
yards long.**

286

The River Eden, to the right of
the line, is joined here by the
River Eamont, which flows out
of Ullswater, 9 miles away on
the edge of the Lake District.

287

The skyline to the left is
dominated for several miles by
Cross Fell, the highest point in
the Pennines at 2930 feet.
South of it are Little Dun Fell
and Great Dun Fell, the latter
with a radar station on its
summit.

288

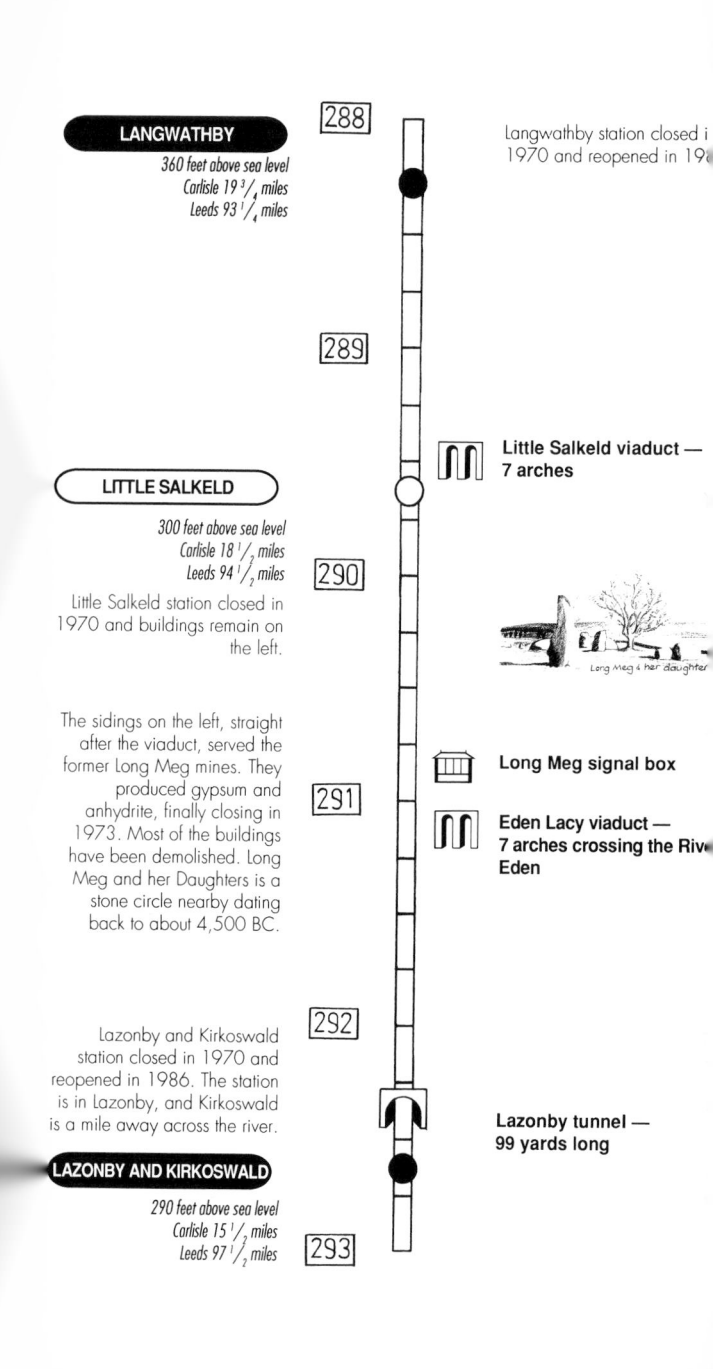

LANGWATHBY

360 feet above sea level
Carlisle 19 ³/₄ miles
Leeds 93 ¹/₄ miles

288

Langwathby station closed i
1970 and reopened in 19

289

LITTLE SALKELD

300 feet above sea level
Carlisle 18 ¹/₂ miles
Leeds 94 ¹/₂ miles

290

Little Salkeld station closed in
1970 and buildings remain on
the left.

Little Salkeld viaduct —
7 arches

Long Meg & her daughter

The sidings on the left, straight
after the viaduct, served the
former Long Meg mines. They
produced gypsum and
anhydrite, finally closing in
1973. Most of the buildings
have been demolished. Long
Meg and her Daughters is a
stone circle nearby dating
back to about 4,500 BC.

291

Long Meg signal box

Eden Lacy viaduct —
7 arches crossing the Riv
Eden

292

Lazonby and Kirkoswald
station closed in 1970 and
reopened in 1986. The station
is in Lazonby, and Kirkoswald
is a mile away across the river.

Lazonby tunnel —
99 yards long

LAZONBY AND KIRKOSWALD

290 feet above sea level
Carlisle 15 ¹/₂ miles
Leeds 97 ¹/₂ miles

293

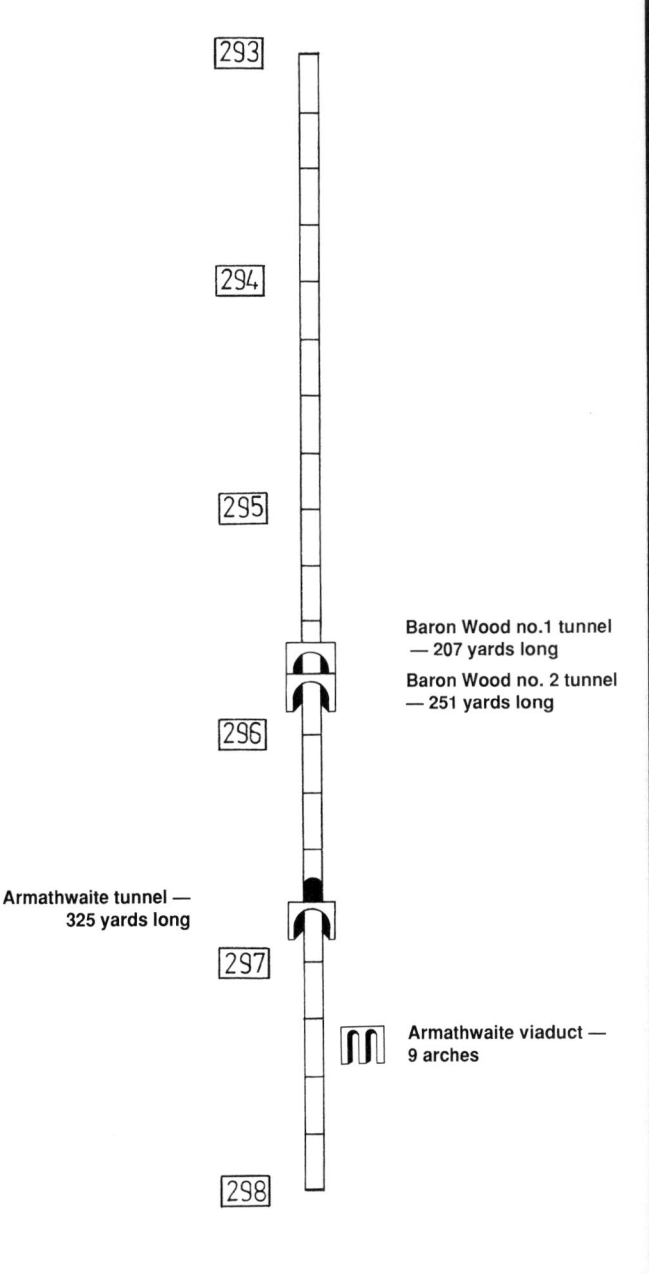

293

294

295

Baron Wood no.1 tunnel
— 207 yards long

Baron Wood no. 2 tunnel
— 251 yards long

296

Armathwaite tunnel —
325 yards long

297

Armathwaite viaduct —
9 arches

298

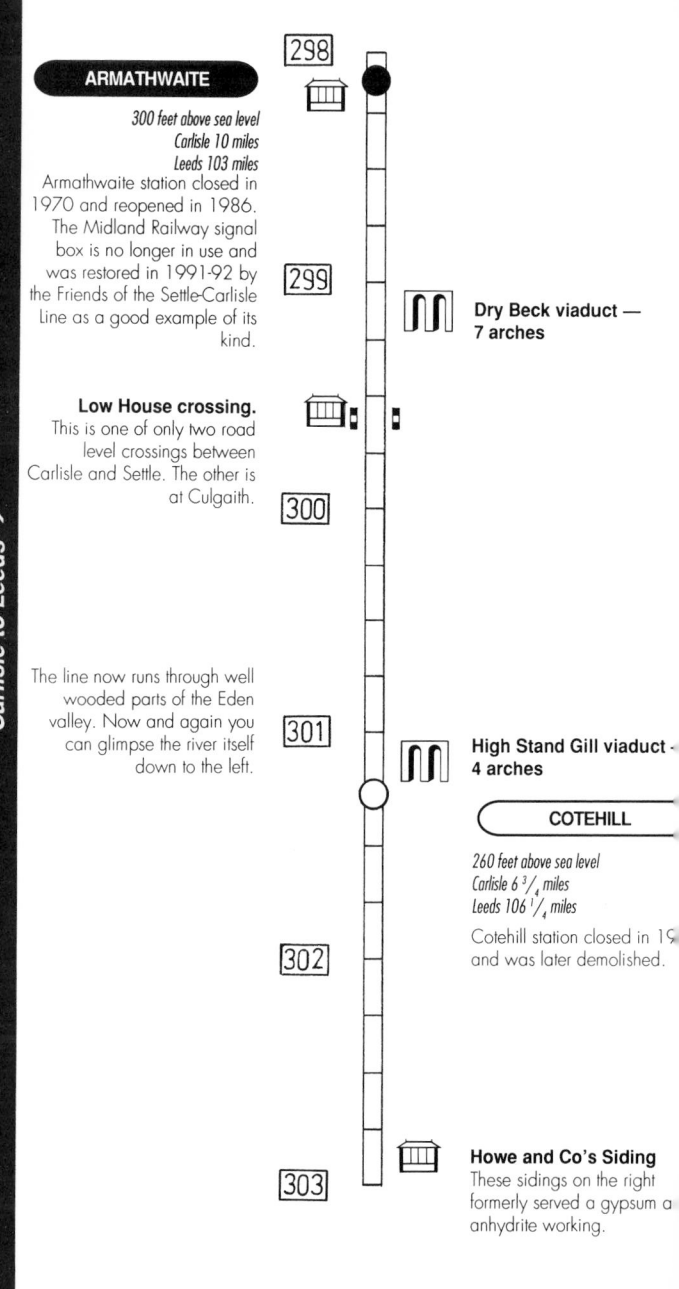

298

ARMATHWAITE

300 feet above sea level
Carlisle 10 miles
Leeds 103 miles
Armathwaite station closed in 1970 and reopened in 1986. The Midland Railway signal box is no longer in use and was restored in 1991-92 by the Friends of the Settle-Carlisle Line as a good example of its kind.

299

Dry Beck viaduct — 7 arches

Low House crossing.
This is one of only two road level crossings between Carlisle and Settle. The other is at Culgaith.

300

The line now runs through well wooded parts of the Eden valley. Now and again you can glimpse the river itself down to the left.

301

High Stand Gill viaduct – 4 arches

COTEHILL

260 feet above sea level
Carlisle 6 ³/₄ miles
Leeds 106 ¹/₄ miles
Cotehill station closed in 19
and was later demolished.

302

303

Howe and Co's Siding
These sidings on the right formerly served a gypsum a anhydrite working.

IV

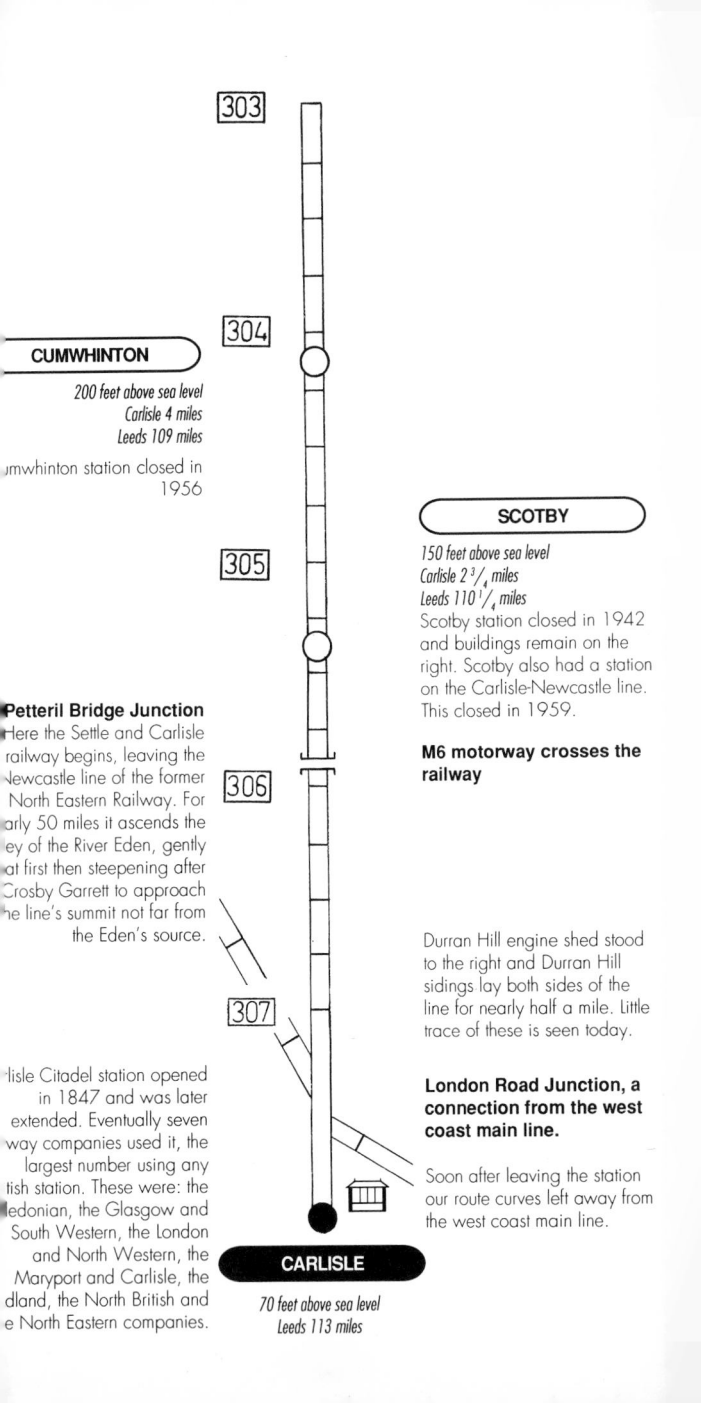

303

304

CUMWHINTON

200 feet above sea level
Carlisle 4 miles
Leeds 109 miles

ımwhinton station closed in
1956

SCOTBY

150 feet above sea level
Carlisle 2 ³/₄ miles
Leeds 110 ¹/₄ miles
Scotby station closed in 1942
and buildings remain on the
right. Scotby also had a station
on the Carlisle-Newcastle line.
This closed in 1959.

305

Petteril Bridge Junction
Here the Settle and Carlisle
railway begins, leaving the
Newcastle line of the former
North Eastern Railway. For
arly 50 miles it ascends the
ey of the River Eden, gently
at first then steepening after
Crosby Garrett to approach
he line's summit not far from
the Eden's source.

**M6 motorway crosses the
railway**

306

Durran Hill engine shed stood
to the right and Durran Hill
sidings lay both sides of the
line for nearly half a mile. Little
trace of these is seen today.

307

**London Road Junction, a
connection from the west
coast main line.**

Soon after leaving the station
our route curves left away from
the west coast main line.

lisle Citadel station opened
in 1847 and was later
extended. Eventually seven
way companies used it, the
largest number using any
tish station. These were: the
ledonian, the Glasgow and
South Western, the London
and North Western, the
Maryport and Carlisle, the
dland, the North British and
e North Eastern companies.

CARLISLE

70 feet above sea level
Leeds 113 miles

Carlisle to Leeds

For instructions on how to use this guide
please refer to page 13 in the
Leeds to Carlisle section.